Islam in Our Midst:
The Challenge to Our Christian Heritage

Islam in Our Midst: The Challenge to Our Christian Heritage

Published in the United States by Isaac Publishing
6729 Curran Street, McLean VA 22101

Unless otherwise stated, all Quranic references are taken from A. Yusuf Ali's *The Holy Quran: Text, Translation and Commentary*, Leicester: The Islamic Foundation, 1975. They are given as the *sura* (chapter) number followed by the number of the verse within the *sura*. Verse numbers may vary slightly between different translations of the Quran, so if using another version it may be necessary to search in the verses just preceding or just following the number given here to find the verse cited.

Library of Congress Control Number: 2011935483
ISBN 978-0-9825218-5-4
Printed in the United States of America

Islam in Our Midst:
The Challenge to Our Christian Heritage

1 | Understanding the Public Square Since 9/11

"In coming to understand anything we must reject the facts as they are for us in favour of the facts as they are."[1]
"C.S. Lewis believed that life and thought were to conform to the plumb line of truth. Truth was not to be bent to fit either convenience or cultural and personal norms."[2]

The role of religion in the public square has again become one of the key issues that animates debate and inflames passions. Few now believe that religion has "died" as a political and social force, though some such as Richard Dawkins wish that this were the case. This book will try to come to terms with the burning question of what role religion does and should have in the wider world. It will assess this both from the Christian perspective and also (particularly in chapters 2 and 3) from the perspective of the rise of Islam, which has brought many unique challenges, forcing us to reassess the way religion is seen in public life. The final chapter will explore how Christians should respond, both to marginalization in the public square and to the rise of Islam throughout the world and particularly to its increasing influence in the West.

This first chapter focuses on three interrelated issues. First, it looks at how Christians fit into the public square, what their role can and should be. Secondly, it assesses some of the changes taking place in the U.S.A. and how these have impacted both the Church and America's[3] sense of itself. Finally, it examines the challenge of Islam, and how America's changing identity is influencing the way Islam is being approached by both the secular establishment and by Christians.

Religion and national identity

Describing a national or cultural identity can be difficult. Observers sometimes struggle to get to the heart of what makes a particular nation or culture tick, to its fundamental driving force. In the West and elsewhere almost every country has had periods of introspection and internal conflict, when its people re-examine who they are or who they should be. The U.S.A. seems to me to be going through one of these periods of introspection now, and, as always, such a period is marked by an increase of confusion and a loss of confidence.

Among the key cultural and national drivers for America is religion. Historically religion has been an important factor in the development of most nations, exercising a profound influence on their culture. In this respect, religion is almost always one of the key drivers of national identity.

Christianity has always been a fundamental part of America's identity and continues to be so today. Although the number of Americans defining themselves as Christians has declined over recent years, church attendance has remained more stable than in Europe, which has experienced a steep decline in church attendance since the late 19th century.

America's religious identity is also framed in the separation of church and state and in recognition of the crucial distinction between the two. In the Alexis de Tocqueville admired the way Americans were able to combine the spirit of religion with the spirit of liberty. By rejecting state establishment, Americans never experienced the problems of clerical power and were able to develop a robust pluralism in which the various Christian churches pursued religious orthodoxy as voluntary associations on roughly equal terms, albeit that reformed Protestant churches had an historical advantage.

The question of conscience and obedience

One of the key differences between the approach to religion in the American tradition and the approach in the British tradition lies in their differing interpretations of the relationship a Christian should have to the state.

The American tradition of Presbyterianism was important in justifying the rebellion against the British because it argued that obedience was first to God, and if rulers were unjust they could be justly opposed. John Locke expressed the concept in philosophical and political terms as "the consent of the governed." If the state compelled one against one's conscience, or interfered in matters of individual belief, there was a moral basis, grounded in God, for resisting its authority. The separation of church and state followed easily from this position. State interference in religion was anathema. It was unacceptable that the state should dictate to Christians how they should worship and what they should believe. The U.S. constitution codified freedom of expression and belief in America, which has been essential to maintaining religious liberty.

In most European countries the state has long been active in the religious life of the nation. Indeed many European countries have an officially sanctioned denomination. Supporters of this tradition see it as vital to maintaining the particular religious identity of a given nation. However, it has caused enormous problems for European nations, as there have been huge changes in the religious makeup of these countries, particularly with the rise of Islam.

One of the areas of difficulty is the desire of the state to influence and control religious expression. In Britain a recent example of this was the Incitement to Religious Hatred bill. This legislation as originally drafted would have allowed for the imposition of a jail sentence on anyone who was convicted of saying something that could stir up religious hatred. The loose wording of early drafts of this legislation meant that a criticism of Muhammad, for example, could have led to a prison sentence. It would have effectively excluded Christians from the public square. After a long struggle the bill was passed, but the Government was forced to accept two important amendments that removed the dangers to free speech. The Government lost on this issue by a single vote, because Prime Minister Tony Blair had gone home and was not present to vote in the House of Commons.

There has been some movement in the U.S.A. to begin to police religious thought and religious expression. Senator Ted Kennedy sponsored a so-called "Hate Crimes Bill" in 2009, which is in committee at the time of writing. Christians have voiced concern that this bill (S.909; in the House H.R. 1913), which prescribes severe penalties for those committing crimes for religious reasons, could have the effect of severely limiting the free discussion of religious issues.

Meanwhile, in several institutions, especially universities, a host of regulations have severely impacted the right to express opinions about religions freely. Well-intentioned laws and regulations meant to prevent religious conflict are easily manipulated to clamp down on religious expression. Clearly Christians must have freedom to enter the public square when they feel guided to do so, without the state preventing them; any other situation prohibits their freedom of religious expression. However, Christians must take great care when they do enter the public square, as they are representing God and their faith. They are wise to make their case on the basis of common grace and moral reasoning, using natural law (general revelation).

What can Christians do? How powerful are Christians? How influential can they be? If Christians want to influence the public square, how are they able to do this? Reason and revelation are conjoined in this matter, as they are in the life and mind of a Christian. As a citizen of a political community and a citizen of God's kingdom, she or he is engaged in both simultaneously, yet with the understanding that the temporal is informed and exceeded by what is eternal and spiritual. Recognizing the nature of human beings and the larger world, the Christian is devoted to God and to His way of redemption in Christ, and the rejection of any utopian or collectivist political ends. No matter the intention, such ideologies inevitably use coercion and deny basic liberties given by God.

The Christian seeks justice, liberty and morality in the political order by upholding the dignity of the individual as inviolable and to be guarded, and at the same time recognizing that individual rights are inseparable from individual responsibility. Thus Romans 13:4 says, "He (the governing authority) is God's servant for your good. But if you do wrong, be afraid, for he does not bear the sword in vain. For he is the servant of God, an avenger who carries out God's wrath on the wrongdoer."

It is crucial that Christians do not accept the fact/value distinction popularized by philosophical materialism, as Truth is first and finally a moral question. Revelation presumes reason, and reason points to revelation. The Christian citizen engages political matters with prudence that is both informed by and exceeded by the Truth of the Gospel.

The power and influence of Christians thus depends upon several factors. First, there is the issue of numbers, in terms of church attendance and of self-identification. Undoubtedly part of the reason politicians in Europe have lost respect for Christianity is declining church attendance and the general lack of a unified and determined position among Christians. In modern democracies politicians are almost always concerned first and foremost with numbers of votes.

Secondly, there is tradition. How strongly is a particular religion seen as being part of the historical culture of a given country? A religion that is seen as part of the fabric of a particular national culture will have influence beyond those who regard themselves as followers of the religion.

Thirdly, and perhaps most importantly, there is belief. What do Christians believe and how strongly do they believe it? How clearly do Christians articulate their ideology and to what extent do they live it? How rooted is their ideology in Biblical fundamentals and how willing are they to avoid short-term compromises that could undermine Christianity in the long term?

In all these areas American Christians apparently have reason to be optimistic, especially compared to their European counterparts. American Christians continue to be well placed to have some influence in the public square, and they can be pivotal in influencing approaches to issues such as the rise of Islam and politically driven Islamic ideologies. However, an underlying cultural shift is gradually undermining the influence that American Christians can have.

Cultural shift

Since the Second World War the West has experienced

massive cultural change, as non-Christian worldviews have become more prominent. Many people have moved away from their Judeo-Christian heritage into various cultural and moral alternatives and ultimately to hard secularism or postmodernism. This shift has led to a radical alteration in the moral basis of Western society and civilization. Undoubtedly some of these trends have accelerated since 9/11, with cultures and institutions disintegrating and government power expanding.

Hard secularism

One of the most important developments has been widespread anti-Christianity, also known as "hard secularism." Despite its professed commitment to tolerance, hard secularism is fundamentally intolerant of Christianity and of moral norms derived from the Bible. It has homed in on Western guilt and shame about two destructive world wars, colonialism, racism and the Holocaust in order to scapegoat theistic religion, especially Christianity, obscuring the fact that the terrible wars and genocides of the 20th century were largely caused by non-religious, secular ideologies such as Fascism, Nazism and atheistic Marxism. At the same time, postmodernism has promoted intellectual and moral relativism, along with a deconstruction of the concepts of truth and knowledge that seeks to undermine Christianity's ultimate truth-claims or even the basis for considering them.

Hard secularism derives from the Enlightenment view that humanity can define itself without reference to God and that reason is the only proper basis of knowledge. As reason came to be defined as equivalent to science and science equivalent to philosophical materialism, it became, as the philosopher and scientist Daniel Dennett described it, a universal acid to just about every traditional concept.

Hard secularism is distinct from soft secularism in that the latter is a political position that favors the religious impartiality of the state and civil society. No religious (or non-religious) position is to be imposed or given privileged status; religious freedom is to be guaranteed, and no one is to suffer discrimination on the grounds of religious belief. Soft secularism is a means of accommodating diverse religious viewpoints within an integrated society. While Christianity is fundamentally opposed to hard secularism, some Christians support soft secularism.

Political correctness and guilt

Political correctness and guilt about the West and its history are widespread. For many they are a generalized posture of moral narcissism and for others a tool for gaining and holding moral and political standing. In a speech in Cairo in 2009 President Obama seemed to accept Western guilt for tensions with the Muslim world and affirmed the myth of Muslims as victims of the West. He spoke of "colonialism that denied rights and opportunities to many Muslims, and a Cold War in which Muslim-majority countries were too often treated as proxies without regard to their own aspirations. Moreover, the sweeping change brought by modernity and globalization led many

Muslims to view the West as hostile to the traditions of Islam." Colonialism, Cold War, modernity and globalization are all products of the West for which Obama sought to apologize to Muslims. He appeared to imply that their hostile attitude to the West is understandable and legitimate, given that the West is the cause of all their troubles.

This politically correct disposition seems to have overrun much of the American establishment, where the desire is always to avoid offending Muslims, even if this gets in the way of telling the truth. Particularly problematic is the influence these attitudes have had on those who are supposed to know exactly what is happening, such as the security services. An overt political correctness has arisen amongst some of the American establishment, which has led them to go to nearly absurd lengths to deny the religious motivations of Islamic terrorists. Indeed, terms such as "Islamic terrorism", "Islamist terrorism" and "jihad" are being excised from the lexicon because they are deemed to anger Muslims and increase tensions with the wider Muslim world.

Politically correct approaches often present a sanitized view of Islam, ignoring its terrorist forms, playing down the place of Islamism and emphasizing the guilt of the West. They offer Islamists a privileged platform in the media and in academic centers, calling any criticism of Islam "Islamophobic" and thereby silencing not only dissent but even discussion. The concept of "Islamophobia" is becoming familiar in the public discourse, with Time magazine's August 2010 cover story asking, "Is America

Islamophobic?" If one cannot examine or discuss Islam critically, and all criticism and rebuttal of Islam is deemed "Islamophobic," is there any wonder that Newsweek ran a cover story in February 2009 by its senior editor, Fareed Zakaria (a Muslim), entitled, "Learning to Live with Radical Islam"?

Multiculturalism

An important trend in recent American history that is also profoundly impacting the significance of Christianity in the public sphere is that of multiculturalism. The U.S.A. has been tremendously successful in integrating different nationalities and cultures into a combined identity. However, the recent obsession with identity politics has threatened to undermine this success.

According to Arthur Schlesinger:

> The genius of America lies in its capacity to forge a nation from peoples of remarkably diverse racial, religious, and ethnic origins. It has done so because democratic principles provide both the philosophical bond of union and practical experience in civic participation. The American Creed envisages a nation composed of individuals making their own choices and accountable to themselves, not a nation based on inviolable ethnic communities. The Constitution turns on individual rights, not on group rights. Law, in order to rectify past wrongs, has from time to time

(in my view properly so) acknowledged the claims of groups; but this is the exception, not the rule.[4]

This is now being threatened by groups that demand special status as they find their identity not in being American but in their particular group. Throughout the history of America most groups (such as Irish, Germans, Jews, and up to now, Mexicans) have identified themselves as Americans even as they delighted in their heritage. However, identity politics is being pushed to extremes in some cases, and this threatens cohesion and could undermine America's sense of identity.

Schlesinger quotes Theodore Roosevelt:

> The one absolutely certain way of bringing this nation to ruin, of preventing all possibility of its continuing to be a nation at all would be to permit it to become a tangle of squabbling nationalities, an intricate knot of German-Americans, Irish-Americans, English-Americans, French-Americans, Scandinavian-Americans, or Italian-Americans, each preserving its separate nationality.

Schlesinger adds that now "we must add a few more nationalities to T.R's brew."

The Heritage Foundation's Statement of Purpose suggests the chief challenge facing the republic is "a pervasive doubt about the core principles that define America and ought to inform our politics and policy."

Lack of self-confidence in the U.S.A.

A trend that appeared after 9/11 and has gradually gained momentum is a growing despair and a lack of confidence. This seems to me to have been influenced by the long delay in apprehending Osama bin Laden, the limited success in Iraq and the problems in Afghanistan, the unexpected resentment towards America from some parts of the world, and the financial crisis. There are growing self-criticism, especially from Hollywood, and America's lack of self-confidence is facilitating those who wish to undermine America's Christian identity. It is also causing anxiety and tension, which are polarizing debates and sometimes leading to extreme responses to the challenges that America faces. This sense of uncertainty and lack of identity could go one of two ways. It could either lead to the nation's reasserting its old confidence, or it could lead to its opening itself up for other forces to enter and exploit its predicament. One such entity is Islam.

Interfaith dialogue

Most Christians are aware of the challenge posed by the resurgence of Islam across the world, and many have sought to engage with the Muslim world, though often with a degree of naivety. Christian leaders have attempted to come to an understanding with their Muslim counterparts in a continuing process of "interfaith dialogue," characterized in particular by the Yale Common Word Conference in July 2008. These efforts at finding "common ground" run the risk of undermining Christian theological fundamentals and presenting all religions as being equally valid revelations from God.

The U.S. Government has acted as a facilitator for interfaith dialogue. As with the many other sectors where government is expanding its role, federal and local governments are increasingly utilizing elements of religion in furthering their policies. "Partnering" with religious leaders and organizations has begun the process of, in effect, officially encouraging and prioritizing the necessity for relations between various faith communities. In February 2009, at the outset of the Obama administration, the White House opened a newly-named Office of Faith-Based and Neighborhood Partnerships. The new office, an expansion of the Bush administration's Office of Faith-Based Initiatives, outlined four key priorities upon which it would focus, one of which is to "work with the National Security Council to foster interfaith dialogue with leaders and scholars around the world." The priority of interfaith action and "outreach" is not unique to the office, however, but something being put into place at nearly every level of government.

Numerous dialogue programs have been organized by local interfaith organizations and councils of churches. There are two major academic centers providing programs focused on Muslim-Christian relations. The first is Hartford Seminary in Connecticut, which has specialized in the study of Islam and Muslim-Christian relations for many years. The second is The Center for Muslim-Christian Understanding (CMCU), founded at Georgetown University in 1993. Through research, publications, and academic and community programs, it seeks to improve relations between the Muslim world and the West as well as enhance understanding of Muslims in the West.

In 2005, the CMCU received a $20 million gift from Prince Alwaleed Bin Talal of Saudi Arabia in order to strengthen and expand its many programs; its full name is now Prince Alwaleed Bin Talal Center for Muslim-Christian Understanding. But what will be the price to academia? There is the old adage that he who pays the piper calls the tune. Can our academic institutions possibly maintain their integrity in the face of these vast sums of money, which are clearly intended to shape academic debate and research? Already in the UK it has become virtually impossible to criticize Islam in academic institutions. This is particularly worrying in the case of Georgetown and Harvard, both of which are prominent in educating future leaders, civil servants, diplomats and government workers.

A Leadership Group on U.S.-Muslim Engagement was set up, which includes high-ranking bipartisan leaders from politics, religion and business. Its brief was to pursue engagement with the Muslim world based on "common-ground" ideology and chart new directions to further this goal. Among its many recommendations was a dramatic expansion of interfaith dialogue initiatives. It urges that highly visible and well publicized interfaith events be held in the U.S., the Middle East and Asia to promote mutual respect based on shared religious values and to educate the public, but to what end? Is this merely another aspect of *dawa*, Islamic mission to bring about Islamic transformation?

Multi-faith and an American seminary

It is instructive and sobering to consider a case study of a well-known American seminary, to see how sharply different ideas about Christian outreach and dialogue with Islam are playing out. Hartford Seminary in Connecticut, one of America's oldest theological schools, was founded in 1834 by Calvinists who left Yale College to found a new institution of Christian learning. In the early decades of the 20th century, Hartford was a leading institution in the evangelization of Muslims. Samuel M. Zwemer (1867-1952), the famous missionary to Muslims, wrote:

> We hope to point out… the true solution to the Moslem problem, namely the evangelization of Moslems and to awaken sympathy, love and prayer on behalf of the Moslem world until its bonds are burst, its wounds are healed, its sorrows removed and its desires satisfied in Jesus Christ.[5]

In 1911, Zwemer founded an academic quarterly titled *The Moslem World*, which offered information on Islam and was a forum for mission strategy among Muslims. He served as its editor for 36 years, and then handed the responsibilities of running it over to Hartford Seminary on the condition that they remain in the same spirit of evangelism and commitment to evangelical truth.

One of the lecturers at Hartford at the turn of the 20th century was the Scotsman Duncan Black Macdonald (1863-1943), who taught Arabic and Islam. A highly respected scholar of Islam, Macdonald held that the seminary students must learn the language and theological heritage of Islam if they were to be successful in evangelizing Muslims. Macdonald's principles, controversial in his own time, later became an important part of Hartford's missionary training. However, the results may not have been what he anticipated, because, in the words of the current Hartford president, Heidi Hadsell, "The missionaries that we sent were coming home saying [Muslims] already believe in God. What we need is dialogue between Muslims and Christians."

Thirty years after Macdonald's death, in 1973, Hartford created the Duncan Black Macdonald Center for the Study of Islam and Christian-Muslim Relations. Its mission is to nurture Christian-Muslim understanding. In 1998, the Center hired Ingrid Mattson, a Canadian-born convert to Islam with a doctorate in Islamic studies from the University of Chicago, to direct the chaplaincy program. Mattson is also the first female president of the Islamic Society of North America, the largest Muslim organization in the United States, which was intended to be "a nucleus for the Islamic Movement in North America."[6] In 2000 an Islamic chaplaincy program was launched at Hartford to train Muslims for chaplaincy roles in the American military. The number of students taking the Islamic chaplaincy training has steadily increased since then. How ironic that today, Muslims make up 35 percent of the student body at Hartford Seminary, an institution which was established to train Christians to evangelize Muslims.

The case of Hartford Seminary shows how the laudable desire to understand Islam and Muslims has brought a Calvinist organization with a strong missionary emphasis to the point of using its resources to train and equip Muslims to strengthen their fellow-Muslims in the Islamic faith. There is a danger that this story will be eventually replicated throughout the Church in the U.S.A.

Learning from others' mistakes? Islam in Europe

Later chapters will explore the challenge of Islam more thoroughly, but at this point a few observations are in order about its impact in Europe. Otto von Bismarck wrote, "A fool learns from his mistakes, but a truly wise man learns from the mistakes of others." This is good advice for American Christians when they consider what has happened in Europe.

Europe's challenge is partially one of demographics. Muslim populations are growing much faster than non-Muslim ones owing to continued migration, higher birth rates and conversions. Many Muslim leaders have expressed their vision of an Islamic Europe in the foreseeable future, achieved through such population shifts. Bernard Lewis predicted in July 2004 that Muslims would form a majority in Europe by the end of the 21st century.[7]

For now, Muslims are still a minority in the West, but their growth rate has been dramatic. In Western Europe there were only about 50,000 Muslims in 1900. By 1970 the number had grown to 3-4 million, and by 2008 it exceeded 25 million.

- Forty per cent of Rotterdam's population is Muslim
- Brussels is one-third Muslim
- Muslims comprise a quarter of both Marseilles' and Malmo's populations
- An estimated 20 per cent of inner London's population is Muslim
- Birmingham's population is 15 per cent Muslim
- A tenth of both Paris and Copenhagen's populations is Muslim

However, for Europeans the challenge is not just one of demographics. Islamists (those who aggressively press the political claims of Islam) have sought to change all aspects of European society. They are politically aware and ambitious. They aim gradually to Islamise Europe through influencing politics, society, the law, finance, education and other spheres. Their strategy to achieve this is already bearing fruit, and there are fears that the changes in Europe are becoming difficult to reverse.

Clearly the American situation is significantly different from that of Europe. Of course the most significant group transforming America is Latino immigrants rather than Muslims. Indeed, the size of the Muslim population in the U.S.A. is not yet significant, and its size has often been exaggerated in the past. However, the impact of the Muslim community in America, particularly that of Islamists, is still in many ways similar to that in Europe, though as yet on a smaller scale. As a group they punch above their weight in terms of influence in media and politics. As chapter 3 will show in more detail, Islamists have aimed to influence every aspect of American society, including the political, financial, social, legal and educational spheres. In some respects Islamists have achieved victories, both in the public square and in the Church. Furthermore, Islamists are gaining dominance within the American Muslim community. During his recent survey of over a hundred mosques in America, Akbar Ahmed noted the continuing failure of traditionalist Muslim leaders to assert themselves against Islamists.[8]

The goal of Islamists is summarized in the stark words of Omar Ahmed, co-founder of the influential Council on American-Islamic Relations (CAIR) and Former President of the Islamic Association for Palestine:

> Islam isn't in America to be equal to any other faith, but to become dominant... The Koran, the Muslim book of scripture, should be the highest authority in America, and Islam the only accepted religion on Earth.[9]

Some Christians in the West have seemingly submitted to the aggressive Muslim discourse. Their acute sense of guilt has blinded their eyes to the real nature of Islam. Many Church leaders seem embarrassed when presenting Christian perceptions, yet present Islam to their congregations and to the general public in idealized, utopian terms. They adopt a protective stance towards Muslims, ignoring their involvement in riots and violence. They identify with Muslims suffering in conflicts in Bosnia, Kashmir or Palestine, protest at Western states' involvement in the invasion of Afghanistan and Iraq, but ignore the suffering of Christian minorities in Muslim states such as Sudan, Saudi Arabia, Indonesia or Iraq. They have a deep desire to be fair to Muslims and to listen to their case, with the result that Muslims are given ample opportunities to speak at various Christian gatherings and churches and to advocate the Muslim agenda across the Christian spectrum.

Islamists have been greatly facilitated by the underlying currents within society and the Church, discussed above: political correctness, emphasis upon identity politics, guilt, self-hatred, relativism, the push towards "hard secularism," and the rejection of fundamentals. These attitudes do not encourage engagement with Islamism as an ideology or a careful and sensible critique of Islam as a religion, both of which are necessary and can be achieved without relinquishing Christian love for Muslims as people. Blindly to ignore the fact of Islamism, or to shy away from meaningful discussion of Islam, is in fact a profound disservice to Muslims and Christians alike.

If the U.S.A. is not confident in its identity and its Christian heritage, it will struggle to face the challenge of Islam and Islamism in a way that is both confident and effective. Europe is already forgetting what it means to European. America must not in its turn forget what it means to be American. Any uncertainty about American identity leaves a void that Islamists can and will exploit.

Going to extremes?

One feature of the American debate is its polarization and the sometimes extreme rhetoric toward the challenges the nation faces. The mosque being built near Ground Zero has generated a major furor. The reasons for supporting it are clearly expressed in the overt political correctness of some of the establishment, the obsession with "multi-faith" projects, and the arrogance of establishment figures such Michael Bloomberg and President Barack Obama who are supporting the project on the grounds of "religious freedom" and supposed public benefit, despite the opposition of nearly seven out of ten New Yorkers.[10] This seeming lack of consideration for the genuine concerns of ordinary Americans has provoked a significant backlash. However, the subsequent threats by Pastor Terry Jones to burn the Qur'an and the frenzied reaction of others to this mosque proposal have been equally inappropriate, resulting in further danger for some Christians already experiencing persecution or vulnerable to it.

The Ground Zero mosque proposal led many American Christians to reconsider what they had been told about Islam, and in particular to consider more seriously some of the bellicose parts of Islamic doctrine. Awareness of these dangers has been growing. However, the attempt to engage in public debate by those who are concerned about Islamism has sometimes sadly demonstrated a lack of Christian concern and love for others. Indeed, the level of chauvinism and hatred of others that is sometimes displayed makes it too easy for critics to dismiss opposition to Islamism as "Islamophobia." It is too reminiscent of unfortunate traditions of racism that have attached themselves to fringes of American Protestantism in the past. When Pastor Jones threatened to burn the Qur'an, those who were immediately threatened were Christians living in Muslim countries. The claim that Jones was behaving in a way which is "un-American" actually holds some weight in light of American traditions of religious liberty and tolerance.

The American debate desperately needs voices in the middle between these extremes: those who can show awareness of the challenge that Islamism brings by making arguments that are driven by facts, not by hyperbole, who can be critical without hating, who are prepared to stand up to protect America's Christian identity without resorting to base racism or xenophobia, who hold true to Biblical fundamentals and show Christian love to all – especially their enemies. Christians still have considerable influence in American society compared to their European counterparts, and they can have a critical impact upon how America responds to the challenge of Islam and Islamism as well as on how America as a country interacts with the Muslim world.

2| Worldviews: Western and Non-Western

This chapter will outline the difference between Western and non-Western worldviews. It will then go on to focus in particular on the Islamic worldview in different contexts and seek to provide a framework for understanding the aims and motivations of different Muslim groups and communities.

It is natural for those seeking to understand Islam from the West to assume that others see the world as they do and to use their own Western-centric values and outlooks. But others can have profoundly different worldviews, and in order to see and understand those views, one must understand one's own worldview as well. Only by first knowing the cultural aspects that influence one's own life can one first grasp the fact that other cultures are fundamentally different from one's own and then try to understand them.

Many of the core lessons in cultural awareness were first learned by missionaries, who had no choice but to learn the target culture in its entirety in order to influence it. In their unique role, missionaries understood before many others did that worldviews can differ substantially from one another. Indeed, those engaged in trying to influence "hearts and minds" would be well advised to consult some of the literature that missionaries have produced, showing how they managed to communicate the Gospel in different ways to completely different cultures across the world.

What is culture and what are worldviews?

Culture is a complex concept and has been the subject of numerous definitions. As Raymond Williams put it, "Culture is one of the two or three most complicated words in the English language."[11] Some definitions of culture have critically underestimated the importance of human behavior and values. The U.S. Department of Defense and NATO, for example, define culture as merely "a feature of the terrain that has been constructed by man. Included are such items as roads, buildings, and canals; boundary lines; and, in a broad sense, all names and legends on a map."[12]

The following definition is to be preferred, because it embraces a far broader range of human activity and attitudes:

> Culture is that complex whole which includes knowledge, belief, art, morals, law, custom and any other capabilities and habits acquired by human beings as members of society.
>
> In its broadest sense, culture refers to the whole range of human activities which are learned and not instinctive, and which are transmitted from generation to generation through various learning processes.

Culture in this wider and more accurate sense can be seen as an integrated system of:

- Beliefs (about God or reality or ultimate meaning)
- Values (about what is true, good, beautiful or normative)
- Customs (how to behave, relate to others, dress etc.)
- Institutions that express these beliefs, values and customs (government, law, places of worship, education, health, etc.)

At the center of any culture is a worldview: a specific way of seeing the world and of seeing one's place in it. Religion has a central role in many cultures in shaping the core worldview. For many people, religion provides a structure by which they can understand the world and their place within it. Religion cannot be overestimated as the key cultural reference point in many non-Western cultures.

In pre-modern society religion typically takes a dominant role in shaping culture. Indeed, in pre-modern societies religion is often regarded as being part of everyday life, and the separation between the material world and the spiritual world is not clear. Often the supernatural is accepted as real and pervasive. The "other world" is not just a matter of belief and doctrine; it impinges on the everyday life of ordinary beings. Religion and culture can become so tightly entwined that they are almost inseparable, with the boundaries between them becoming unclear. In many modern, non-Western contexts, religion remains the dominant influence on culture.

There are other important influences on culture, including the physical environment, economic factors, and attempts to shape culture by those in political power. History can be strongly influential on many cultures. Historic events, particularly the history of military victories and (perhaps even more importantly) defeats, can have a huge influence on contemporary attitudes, even if these events happened centuries ago. Other crucial historic events, such as natural disasters, plagues and revolutions, can have powerful cultural resonances for future generations.

So what then do these culturally-specific worldviews influence? The answer is "almost everything." They produce different ways of thinking, communicating and behaving. Divergent worldviews produce vastly different societies, with contrasting values and different priorities.

The secular American worldview

The U.S.A. is both a unity and a diversity. It is a unity in that it has an over-arching culture based upon a number of factors to be considered below. It is a diversity in that within the whole there exist varieties of races, cultures, religions and worldviews. In describing aspects of the American worldview (many of which are also part of other Western worldviews) that combine to form a distinct culture, it is necessary to generalize from part of that diversity. So the worldview described here is principally that of the East Coast elite, which will be considerably different from, say the worldview of the Mid-West.

First, American culture is dichotomous; that is, it divides life into diametrically opposed compartments. American–and, by extension, Western–culture divides the world into separate facets that it strives to compartmentalize and keep as separate as possible. This involves dissecting almost every conceivable aspect of life. American culture is characterized by numerous examples of these divides, such as military vs. civilian, scientific vs. spiritual, rational vs. mystical, natural vs. supernatural, cultural vs. supra-cultural, human vs. divine, this-worldly vs. otherworldly, empirical vs. intuitive.

The dichotomous worldview is perhaps most importantly expressed in the American attitude toward religion and government. For most Americans, the separation of Church and state, a separation that has a long history in America, remains a fundamental value. It began in the 17th century, when Roger Williams established full freedom of religion and a complete separation between Church and state in Rhode Island in 1636. William Penn did the same in Pennsylvania in 1682. Gradually, other states followed suit, especially after the First Amendment of the Constitution in 1791, which codified this separation, with the words: "Congress shall make no law respecting an establishment of religion, or prohibiting the free exercise thereof…"

As an aside, the worldview of Eastern Europeans and Russians is often said to be dichotomous too, but this is more a feature of cultural conflict within a traditional communal society that is being partially modernized, creating anxious debates about whether Russia is or should be Western or Asian, sacred or post-Christian, individualistic or communal, etc. For example, it is often said that Russia can be only one thing or the other and there is rarely any attempt to find middle ground.

A further aspect of this dichotomous worldview is the separation of public and private space. Attempts are made to keep work lives and home lives separate, with work rarely crossing into home life. Though keeping these spheres completely separate is essentially impossible, unlike in communal cultures, attempts are made to define boundaries and stop public and private from flowing into each other. The maintenance of a separate private space is allowed by the dominance in America (and most Western countries) of the single-family house as the main living area, rather than communal homes with parents, extended family or neighbors. It is this availability of private space in the West that makes private lives possible. Indeed the importance of private space impacts upon all areas of behavior.

Another fundamental American characteristic is individualism. American individualism is seen in part as the opportunity to make individual choices without the restrictions that limit people according to their class, religion, or race. Americans historically contrasted the greater opportunities they had compared to Europeans, who were constrained by factors that limited an individual's potential.

Historian James Truslow Adams coined the phrase "American Dream" in his 1931 book *Epic of America*:

> The American Dream is that dream of a land in which life should be better and richer and fuller for every man, with opportunity for each according to ability or achievement. It is a difficult dream for the European upper classes to interpret adequately, also too many of us ourselves have grown weary and mistrustful of it. It is not a dream of motor cars and high wages merely, but a dream of social order in which each man and each woman shall be able to attain to the fullest stature of which they are innately capable, and be recognized by others for what they are, regardless of the fortuitous circumstances of birth or position.[13]

Social factors have promoted American individualism, particularly through the American tradition of home and car ownership. The U.S.A. has unusually high rates of geographic mobility, with individuals and families willing to move thousands of miles in order to find new jobs and opportunities. Though the recent economic downturn has impacted upon this aspect of American culture, undoubtedly decades of constant moving and relocation have helped foster self-sufficient and independent outlooks. However, it is important to emphasize that American individualism does not necessarily entail selfishness; indeed in a recent survey ranking 153 nations on the willingness of their citizens to donate time and money to charity, Australia and New Zealand shared first place, and the United States tied for fifth.

America has a legal tradition that draws upon the concept of natural law, which asserts that certain ideals, values and practices are natural to humanity. Natural law concepts are echoed in the vocabulary of the American Declaration of Independence. An important outcome of America's legal culture is the emphasis upon rights. The U.S. is unique among Western democracies in that it did not emerge gradually out of ancient customs but has a clear historical beginning. From the time of its very conception, the protection of the rights of American citizens was seen as crucial.

Thinkers such as Thomas Paine were influential in establishing the protection of rights as a bastion of American culture. The Bill of Rights symbolizes the centrality of rights in American culture. Rights are crucial in restricting power: the power of the government, the power of the police, the power that citizens can hold over each other. The limitation of power is seen as critical to preventing it from being abused. Rights are also considered crucial in guaranteeing Americans "life, liberty and the pursuit of happiness." This has created a culture where Americans are assertive in knowing the rights and freedoms they have and in demanding that these rights and freedoms are respected and protected. It creates a society where citizens are proactive and ready to engage in the public square and can be easily mobilized.

Another aspect of the American worldview is that it is characterized by immediacy. Different cultures interpret time in different ways. For example, in the U.S. time is conceived of as linear, flowing from past to present to future, while many other cultures see it as cyclical. In the U.S., "time is money," but in others it can be used to reflect a person's worth: the person's status determines how much time is spent with them. Muslim culture, for example, tends to be person-centered rather than time or work-centered. In some cultures, social occasions and appointments do not have fixed beginnings and endings and people are relaxed and flexible about time, frequently turning up late, or not doing something by a promised deadline, depending on the status of the person to whom the promise is made.

The West is considered a "now" culture, with the expectation that wants and desires should be met promptly. Undoubtedly, changes in technology have contributed to this attitude, with delivery of goods and services fulfilled faster and more conveniently. Thanks to huge advances in communications, information can be found and sent extremely quickly. In some ways this "speeding up" of Western culture has led it to become a culture of instant gratification. The Biblical concepts of *chronos* (sequential or chronological time) and *kairos* (the opportune or decisive moment) are increasingly lost, as humans pursue immediate happiness at any cost, unwilling to wait on God and to acknowledge His time.

A good example of differing cultural approaches to time occurred during the second UN peace-keeping mission in Somalia (1993-1996). At first the UN tried to push through agreements that postulated a coercive response if they were not quickly accepted. However, this proved counterproductive and ultimately exacerbated tensions. Eventually the UN peace-keepers changed their negotiating tactics in order to match the slow pace of Somali decision-making, which entails long deliberation and consultations involving hundreds of local tribal leaders and where initial decisions are not seen as final but as a prelude to further discussions. It was only when UN peace-keepers allowed this long-drawn-out process time for completion and did not try to impose their own concepts of time upon the Somalis that an agreement was eventually reached.

The final aspect of the American worldview to be highlighted is the emphasis upon technology. American culture has a fondness for scientific advancement and technological innovation, with iconic generators of technological advancement such as Silicon Valley. It is often suggested that deeply rooted in this affinity for technology is the belief that humans can have mastery over their environment. Also linked to the reverence for technology is scientific materialism, which focuses all of human emphasis and purpose on the here and now. In this view, hope is limited to what can be achieved in this life, and death is the ultimate disaster, a view that can lead to a deep pessimism.

So these various aspects of the American worldview lead to specific ways of behaving, thinking and communicating. They form a useful point of reference when considering other worldviews, particularly the Islamic worldview.

The Islamic worldview

Islam is a multi-faceted and multi-dimensional faith.

While it has a basic simplicity allied to a fundamental unity, its expressions are many and various. The Muslim world is largely made up of traditional Muslims, who are generally peaceful, without any harmful intent or interest in Islamic global strategy. Their primary concern is to live out their lives and personal faith within societies that can offer them the freedom to do so, and where they can seek economic betterment, opportunities for their children and protection for their women within a clearly defined Islamic religious context.

In the U.S., the majority of Muslims come from well-to-do and well-educated backgrounds, in contrast to Muslims in Europe. They have found in the U.S. a home that has offered to them the means of attaining and achieving their economic ends and performing their religious duties, albeit within a secular framework. This has led to a much greater degree of assimilation of Muslims within American society than that of Muslims in Europe. However, as they become more educated in their faith and are increasingly subject to ideological forces and ideas from their homelands or from foreign sources, they find themselves increasingly under pressure, and this is beginning to produce a transformational shift. Some of the forces that are at work in their worldview are described below.

The Islamic worldview is not dichotomous like its American secularist counterpart, and there is no attempt to divide the religious and secular realms. A fundamental doctrine of Islam is the unity of religion (*din*) and state (*dawla*). Islam is thus inherently political. In a very real sense, for

Muslims Islam is the state. Sharia (Islamic law), derived from the Qur'an and other sources, contains a complete social and political order, with regulations not only on personal devotion but also on all elements of legal jurisdiction, political institutions, relations with other states and even military endeavors. The struggle to achieve an "Islamic state" is the central motivation for many radical Islamic groups, some of whom see it as so important that violence and terrorism are justified in seeking to make it a reality.

Religion and politics are thus inseparable in Islam, as explained by S. Abdullah Schleifer:

> Just as there is no political thought separate from religious thoughts, so in at-tawhid[14] shaped consciousness, there is no aspect of religious thought necessarily separate from political thought.[15]

Even a comparatively moderate scholar like the late Zaki Badawi claimed that it is impossible to separate Islam from politics:

> The suggestion of separating Islam from politics would be tantamount to abandoning Islam itself, as there is no separate institution equivalent to the Church for the Muslim religion. To deprive the Muslim community of the support of the political arm of their society to the tenets of their religion is to abolish the religion itself.[16]

As a result, everything Muslims do has, in their view, political connotations. In contrast to the Western and American situation, in which secularism has increasingly marginalized religion, most Muslims are religious, and Islam remains a significant social and political force in all Muslim societies and states, even those that are defined as secular in their constitutions.

A further aspect of the Islamic worldview is the emphasis upon the Muslim community. The worldwide Islamic nation, the *umma*, is a concept of very great importance in Islam. It is the brotherhood of all Muslims, from which non-Muslims are excluded by definition. Consequently, non-Muslims occupy a subordinate position, both socially and legally. The *umma* gives its members a sense of belonging, identity and self-worth. Belonging to a transnational community, which is loyal and protective of its own, can be very attractive to those who are tired of an individualistic culture or alienated by the forces of modernity and globalization.

The communalism of Islam, as opposed to the individualism of American society, leads to a very different attitude to private space and public space. The *umma* is not just a spiritual brotherhood but a physical trans-national nation, and therefore there is little or no concept of private or individual space.

Allegiance to the *umma* transcends all national allegiances. This can create tensions and conflicts for Muslims living in societies such as the U.S. It raises the question of where one's first loyalty lies. Furthermore, ultra-conservative Muslims have the added pressure of living under a non-Muslim ruler when their theology is based on the assumption of Islamic political power being dominant. Islam never developed a theology for a minority situation; its theology was formulated for a situation in which Muslims had political control. As one *hadith* (tradition) says, "Islam rules. It is never ruled."

Nevertheless, within the *umma* there are major fractures that are ethnic, sectarian and ideological. But when under pressure, members of the *umma* will forget their differences and close ranks against the non-Muslims.

Most Muslims stress the doctrine of divine unity (*tawhid*) as the foundation of Islam. The one god of Islam created everything, and all existence issues from his absolute will. The universe is created a unified and harmonious whole, preserved and ordered by this god, who is sovereign and the supreme ruler. The Muslim emphasis on his transcendence leads to a theology that is close to deism. His immanence, the divine presence, is lacking in Islamic theology. This presents a challenge to the U.S., which has increasingly lost a sense of divine transcendence and focuses too much on immanence. One result is that humankind becomes divine and all exists to serve them.

For Muslims, divine unity means there can be only one god-approved law, sharia, and one right political model for human society, as the absolute and indivisible divine unity must be replicated in human society and politics. The existence of a divine law, ordained by the god of Islam, excludes the possibility of any other kind of law, such as natural law or human law. Fundamentalist Muslims increasingly call for the implementation of this doctrine and have a commitment to establish an integrated social and political order on earth that mirrors the divine order in heaven. The impact of Islam and Islamic law in the public space is all important; the concept of a personal devotional life of faith within the private space has little emphasis in mainstream Islam.

As the god of Islam is the only sovereign and legislator in the universe, there can be no competing human sovereignty of people or of parliament. Humans must submit to his revealed law in all areas of life. They cannot legislate; they can merely interpret and apply his law. All independent human legislation is evil. The U.S. concept of a self-governing society with government "of the people, by the people, for the people" would be regarded as heretical. Furthermore, human beings' total submission to the god of Islam and to his law frees them from submission to any other power and places.

A further aspect of divine transcendence and the overriding importance of sharia is the lack of a concept of rights and freedoms within Islam, either for individuals or for communities. Humans are not seen as possessing any rights by virtue of their humanity. Rather, human needs are met by the concept of duty to others. So a hungry Muslim is given food not because he or she has the right to life, but because other Muslims have a duty to care for the Muslim poor. In Christianity, God creates human beings in the divine image (*imago dei*). All human beings are therefore equal, irrespective of race, culture, religion or gender. In

Islam, however, human beings are not created in the divine image, which is why they have no intrinsic worth or rights. Their worth is defined by sharia, according to which men are more valuable than women, and Muslims more valuable than non-Muslims.

The Muslim worldview is also very much shaped by the past, which determines the certainties for today and the patterns for the future. Within that past Muslims focus especially on the "Golden Age" of Islam, that is, the early centuries when Islam and Islamic rule spread across the world with a speed they consider miraculous. Muslims live in a continuum that sees all history as one. Unlike the U.S. and the Western world, which tends not to see history as an interpreter for the present or the future, the Muslim mind finds not just contentment but also meaning by interpreting the present in terms of the past. This can lead to frustration, however, for when the Muslim mind looks outwards it does not see a vast Muslim empire but rather a secular society that has globalized and is now impacting on Muslim societies. When Muslims ask why there should be such a state of affairs, the answer is invariably: "We Muslims have left our god; we have rejected his unity, his sovereignty and his law, and it is only by a return that we can see the former Golden Age of Islam re-established."

Looking back and seeking revival have therefore been constantly recurring themes in Islamic thought, with the expectation that revival will occur at the end of every century. As this hadith puts it:

The Prophet (peace be upon him) said: Allah will raise for this community at the end of every hundred years the one who will renovate its religion for it.[17]

The emphasis on the past and the future, combined with – in fundamentalists at least – a great disdain for modern Western-originated technology, gives Muslims a long-term optimism that is largely lacking from the American secular worldview, with its emphasis on scientific materialism.

Most Muslims accept the traditional Sunni or Shi'a eschatology on the signs of the End Times: the appearance of the Antichrist (*al-Dajjal*), the coming of the Mahdi or the return of the hidden Imam to set up a righteous rule on earth, and the return of Isa (Jesus) as a Muslim to set up his kingdom on earth. For some Muslims, particularly Islamists, these beliefs encourage them to see themselves as engaged in the final battle of the End Time, justifying both separatism and active involvement in world affairs, as well as conspiracy theories and violence. According to the Islamic calendar, the 15th century began in November 1979, and many Muslims believe that the 15th century will see the ultimate victory of Islam. This vision of a new age of Islam, of the ultimate victory of Islam, which shapes their attitudes and lifestyles, contrasts sharply with the American concept of immediacy, where living for today is all important. Of course, for many Christians there is also a strong belief in the Second Coming of Christ and events surrounding his coming. Christians, of course, await not the Muslim Isa but the Biblical Jesus.

Shifts in the Islamic worldview

The Islamic worldview, like all worldviews, is not static but dynamic. While the core beliefs of Muslims do not change rapidly, the changes in interpretation of belief and the subsequent impact on ways of behaving, thinking and communicating can be significant.

The eruption of ideological disputes has been a perennial feature of Islamic history and continues to this day. For example, in the 9th and 10th centuries the Mu'tazilites, who thought that reason should take precedence over revelation, argued with the Ash'arites who argued for the primacy of revelation. Modern debates between liberal reformers, traditionalists and Islamists in some way mirror those debates.

The undoubted shift in worldview among Muslims over recent decades originates in the rapid modernization of Muslim countries. The traditional social structures, formed over centuries, have come under threat from massive migration to the cities and an influx of Western influences. Muslims have reacted in a number of different ways to the challenge of modernity.

First, there are the liberal reformers who seek to adapt Islam to the modern world. They often emphasize that Islamic texts that justify violence should be reinterpreted and the sharia should be modernized. Secondly, traditionalists try to shield their form of Islam from the modern world; this entails separating themselves as much as possible from the Western influences and preserving traditional practices.

Thirdly, there are the Islamists, who respond to modernity by purifying Islam through a return to the original Islamic sources and the model of the Golden Age of Islam. After this purification, they seek to Islamize the modern world by imposing a dominant Islamic system in all areas of society: political, legal and social. The shift to Islamism has the potential to change the Islamic worldview fundamentally if it becomes dominant among Muslims.

Conclusion

The Islamic worldview is fundamentally different from the secular American worldview. Yusuf al-Qaradawi, the popular Muslim cleric and scholar based in Qatar, often defined as "moderate" by Western politicians and media, explicitly rejects secularism as apostasy from Islam because it means abandoning the rule of sharia:

> Since Islam is a comprehensive system of 'Ibadah (worship) and Shari'ah (legislation), the acceptance of secularism means abandonment of Shari'ah, a denial of the Divine guidance and a rejection of Allah's injunctions… the call for secularism among Muslims is atheism and a rejection of Islam. Its acceptance as a basis for rule in place of Shari'ah is a downright apostasy.[18]

The various differences between the Islamic worldview and the secular American worldview may perhaps be summarized as the difference between a holistic view and a dichotomous view. The Islamic worldview is holistic, connecting every aspect of life and faith in a complete system for humankind with religion at the center. The Islamic worldview does not have the separations inherent in the American view. Devotion and politics, past, present and future, are all bound up together. Separating religion from politics is seen as perverse in an Islamic worldview, which views the state as the instrument of God's authority on earth and which has a complete legal structure believed to be divinely inspired.

As much as possible those in charge of policy, both Christian and secular leaders, need to understand that these core differences in worldview often result in radically different attitudes and values. It is also important to note the potentially dangerous shifts currently taking place in the Islamic worldview as Muslims grapple with modernity and many of them try to return to past glories. Undoubtedly, the years ahead will see instability in the Muslim world and a growing crisis of identity for Muslims living in the West. Yet perhaps the greatest challenge for American Christians is that the Islamic worldview is determined by and incorporates suffering and continuous conflict, and the belief that Islam will be ultimately triumphant. By contrast, too many in our society grasp onto empty hopes that lack any unifying vision of the divine. This is turn can lead to growing pessimism. However, it must also be noted that Christian eschatology is still a dominant factor in the U.S., and this carries with it both hope and the final victory of Christ.

3 | The Impact of Islam on Society:
Key Issues for Policy Makers

Muslims started migrating to the West in the latter part of the 19th century in a quest for material well-being, to escape the increasing instability and crises within their homelands, and for other reasons as well. Several waves of large-scale migration from the Muslim world to Western Europe and the United States occurred, primarily after the Second World War.

Initially, most immigrants kept a low religious profile and satisfied their immediate religious needs by building mosques. But others, particularly those in Islamist movements, were organizing at the local, national and international levels. In the late 1970s and 1980s, with the rise of Islamic organizations, the religious self-awareness of Muslims residing in Europe and America awoke. In the U.S., an important catalyst was the formation of the first significant national Muslim organization, the Muslim Student Association (MSA). The MSA had reached out to the many young, affluent Muslim students from overseas who were coming to study in U.S. and Canadian universities in the 1950s and 1960s. Chapters arose at colleges across North America where Muslim students could meet together. The MSA was the recruiting, training and discipleship end of the growing Islamist movement.

At the same time, a massive Saudi-funded effort was underway to produce, translate, publish and distribute Qur'ans and Salafist materials from figures such as Syed Qutb and Abul Ala Maududi throughout the globe, and especially in the West. This went hand in hand with the quest to preserve Islamic identity in the face of an increasingly secular western culture, and a desire to learn more about Islam and establish it within one's own life and within the indigenous non-Muslim society. It was in the 1970s, with the resurgence of Islam and the rapid rise of Islamism backed by oil wealth, that *dawa* (Islamic mission) unfolded in North America and Europe.[19]

In the United States, Muslims still make up a small portion of the overall population. A May 2007 report by the Pew Research Center put the number of Muslims in the U.S.A. at 2.35 million.[20] Other surveys have stated five to seven million, but all the suggested figures are only a tiny percentage of the U.S. population of 300 plus million. (A figure of 2.35 million is only 0.8%, and even one of seven million is only 2.3%.) But as media headlines and the shifting policies and priorities of the U.S. government make clear, this small percentage has a disproportionately large influence. Much of this influence is exerted through national and international Islamic organizations (associations, movements, and official bodies) that identify all American Muslims as part of the larger one-and-a-half-billion collective of Muslims, the *umma*.

Since 9/11 there has been a dramatic change in the perception of Islam by non-Muslims. In the Obama administration and throughout various agencies, Islam is portrayed as a religion of peace and an ally to be engaged in the war against terrorism. There is a tension between those who hold a sanitized view of Islam and those who are concerned about its potential for violence and conflict. Over the same time period, Islam has been growing in self-assertiveness.

Islamic Self-Assertiveness in the West

Societal

Pressure is being exerted for clearly separate Muslim communities and geographical areas across the West. This often entails visible symbols and structures, most of all the prominent building of mosques and attempts to introduce sharia as an alternative legal system.

Throughout the West an Islamic character is being imposed on many inner-city areas, where Muslim social networks are very powerful. This is the case not only in the UK and Europe, but also increasingly within the U.S., in cities such as Detroit and Philadelphia.[21] In part these date back to the arrival in the West of the first generations of Muslims, who, because of poverty, racism and the need for mutual support, lived close together. More recently this process has been encouraged by Islamists who seek to consolidate and increase their control over the community. This has taken shape under the nose of governments, with either their tacit approval or active aid. It creates a growing sense of separation from the wider society and encourages young Muslims to seek their identity in radical Islam.

An example of the pressure for sharia within Muslim communities was seen in 2004 when Somali taxi drivers at the Minnesota airport refused to pick up passengers with seeing-eye dogs or those carrying alcohol on the grounds that their "religious rights have to be respected."

Halal *food*

The Islamic Food and Nutrition Council of America (IFANCA) made a list of 36 different categories of food, drinks, and cosmetics, covering 301 products that meet Islamic religious requirements. The list of giant food industries that have adopted *halal*-compliant food includes Burger King, Coca Cola, Del Monte, Ferrero Rocher, Kentucky Fried Chicken, Kraft, McDonalds, Nestle, Nutella, Pepsi, Pizza Hut, and Wendy's.[22] Zabihah.com provides an online service that directs users to restaurants around the world that provide *halal* food.[23]

IFANCA has been endorsed by government and Islamic organizations such as the USDA, the Malaysian government, the Islamic Committee Office of Thailand, Majelis Ulama Indonesia, Majlis Ugama Islam Singapura, Muslim World League of Saudi Arabia, and the Philippine Halal Association.[24] Undoubtedly, food exporters in the U.S. are interested in exploiting the global Muslim market. The market for *halal* goods is estimated at 2 trillion dollars annually.[25] Muslims in the U.S. alone are estimated to have purchasing power worth $12 billion annually.[26]

The workplace

In repeated incidents, several of which have taken the form of lawsuits, Muslim employees in America have demanded the right to bring their external religious practice, as set down in the sharia, to the workplace. Newark Police Department officers Faruq Abdul-Aziz and Shakoor Mustafa asserted that, according Sunni Islam tradition, not growing a beard is as bad as eating pork. They registered a complaint with the New Jersey Federal District Court claiming a violation of religious freedom when their superior enforced the Department policy of banning beards.[27] A similar claim was made by Zeinab Ali when her employer refused to allow her to wear a head scarf at work.[28]

Such outward religious appearance has been claimed as part of religious practice that employers should have to accommodate. Encouraged by the right to religious freedom in America, Muslims have been making more demands of their employers, such as the flexibility to take time off for Friday prayer, to conduct daily prayers while at work, and to be provided with *halal* food, a prayer area, and an area where they can perform the ablutions required before prayer.[29] CAIR has issued guidelines to law enforcement, health care, prison and educational employers, and employers in general, on how to treat Muslims at a work place and has also focused political action to allow the special treatment of Muslims and influence the media coverage surrounding it.

Education

Western countries have found the issue of education relating to Islam and Muslims particularly challenging. In Great Britain there has been a huge rise in the numbers of Muslim schools, a few of which are publicly funded. These schools have been a particular cause for concern because they have sometimes been forces for separation and, especially in the case of Saudi-funded schools, prone to radicalization.

Islamic schools and *dawa* are spreading within the public school system in the United States as well. Dozens of charter schools throughout the U.S. are run by international Islamic organizations and networks, such as the one headed by Fethullah Gülen. Gülen directs a network of 500-700 Islamic schools around the globe, over 90 of which are within the U.S., where he now lives. Operating as charter schools in California, Texas, Ohio, and seventeen other states, the Gülen academies receive government money but do not have to meet the same requirements as normal public schools nor adopt their curriculum. The schools often present themselves as "science" schools and receive support from both government and private foundations, including the Gates Foundation and other well known "progressive" groups.[30]

The Islamization of knowledge

There is an apparent drive to change basic Western categories of knowledge, bringing them into an Islamic framework. For decades, the major funding for academic chairs in Islam and related studies appears to have been directed toward this purpose. The goal appears to be to influence students and the teaching of academic subjects with Islamist concepts of science, knowledge and religion. Another method is the founding of Islamic think tanks, including research and academic institutions, that can disseminate Islamic views on the integration of all human knowledge into an Islamic system based on the principles of Qur'an and *sunna* and on the legacy of Islamic civilization. Some of these institutions are linked to Islamist movements while presenting a moderate face to their Western audiences. They develop links to Western academia and liberal Christian institutions that tend to cooperate with them because of their academic credentials, unaware of or ignoring their largely undisclosed agendas.

A good example of this may be seen in the work of a major Islamic think tank called the International Institute of Islamic Thought (IIIT). The stated mission of the organization, which was founded in 1981 in Herndon, Virginia, is "the Islamization of knowledge." Towards that aim the Institute has published more than 400 titles and, since 1984, a "scholarly, refereed, quarterly journal." IIIT's work now involves numerous professors, students and academic programs from major universities across the U.S. and the world.

The late Ismail al-Faruqi, a longtime professor at Temple University who was the first director of IIIT and one of its founders, believed that the crisis of the modern world was the crisis of knowledge. This crisis, al-Faruqi thought, could only be cured via a new synthesis of all knowledge in an Islamic epistemological framework.[31]

Al-Faruqi describes this mission in his book, *Islam and Other Faiths*. "It (*din al-fitrah*) gives him the world to reknead and remold in the service of God. To serve God is hence to create culture and civilization. But this is none other than to attain the highest possible self-fulfillment."[32]

James Beverly, author of the book *Islamic Faith in America*, explains in the simplest terms what al-Faruqi and the IIIT's concept of the "Islamization of knowledge" entails:

> Al Faruqi believed emphasizing a liberal arts education apart from religion was harmful, especially to young people. He felt all learning should be captured under the umbrella of Islam – that is, all subjects not just religion, should be presented to Muslim students in accordance with the teachings of Islam.[33]

What are some of the results of this "education" by IIIT and the MSA? The most immediate and obvious results have of course been among Muslims. A description of the present-day Muslim Student Association is provided in a book by Geneive Abdo titled *Mecca and Main Street: Muslim Life in America after 9-11*. The book, it should be noted, is published by Oxford University Press and is in no way critical of Islam or Muslims. Abdo gives a snapshot of the University of Michigan's MSA chapter, which is located near Dearborn, Michigan, home of one of the largest Muslim communities in the U.S. She writes:

> (The members) were either radical Salafis or affiliated with the Hizb ut-Tahrir al-Islami, the Islamic Party of Liberation. The movement, a clandestine, radical Sunni Islamic group that is banned in several countries around the world, advocates the replacement of individual Muslim governments with a single caliphate governed under a strict reading of the sharia. The students who are members of Hizb ut-Tahrir al-Islami share a common creed that calls for strict adherence to the Koran and the rejection of applying human reason and logic when interpreting the Islamic holy texts.[34]

The academic literature and popular materials generated by the IIIT, the MSA and others, which are advancing the "Islamization of knowledge," are not the exception. There is a growing trend, both in the UK and also increasingly in America, for educational materials and textbooks to provide a positive portrayal of Islam and a more negative portrayal of Christianity. History textbooks depict a mythologized Islam. It is invariably peaceful and benign. Its conquests and aggressive wars are airbrushed out. It is presented as a major source of advances in science, medicine and the arts. An example of this is *World History: A Cultural Approach* by Daniel Roselle, which includes this lesson: "Wherever they went, the Moslems brought with them their love of art, beauty and learning. From about the eighth to the eleventh century, their culture was superior in many ways to that of western [*sic*] Christendom." Elsewhere, students learn from Roselle how, under Christian rule, "idols, temples and other material evidences of paganism [were] destroyed."[35] The text also marvels at how, after it was conquered by Muslims, the Spanish city of Cordoba's "streets were solidly paved," unlike in Paris. And lamps were erected, while in London, as the author takes pains to point out, there was not a single public lamp!

Islamic finance

In the last two decades, Islamic financing and banking have seen spectacular growth. Islamic financial products were worth nearly a trillion U.S. dollars by 2010. This is a new phenomenon prompted by the assertion of Islamist movements that Western financial products are inconsistent with sharia. As a result, they have created a range of alternative "sharia-compliant" products, and they are pressuring all Muslims to use them. This is happening despite a controversy amongst Muslims regarding the Quranic prohibition of *riba* and whether this term denotes any kind of interest (as contemporary Islamists claim) or only exploitative interest (the traditional Muslim interpretation, still held by many Muslims today).

The Islamists are rapidly winning their argument and using sharia finance as a tool further to bring about the Islamization of all aspects of society. They are doing so with the help of Western financial institutions, government, media and academics, many of which have backed the founding of Islamic banks and financial institutions in the West. Western governments increasingly support the introduction of this "Islamic finance," hoping to attract investment from the oil-rich Middle East. London has become the main Western center for Islamic finance and investment. In a 2005 survey several Islamic companies indicated that the Great Britain was the most sharia-friendly of all the Western countries.

Sharia finance is growing in the United States as well. More Islamic and conventional banks are offering sharia-compliant mortgages and other products. The Dow Jones Islamic Market Index[SM] includes 69 country indexes, as well as thousands of broad-market, blue-chip, fixed-income and strategy and thematic indexes that have passed rules-based screens for sharia compliance. The indexes are described by Dow Jones as "the most visible and widely-used set of Shari'a-compliant benchmarks in the world," and cover business across "10 broad Industries, 19 Super-sectors, 41 Sectors, and at the most granular level, 114 Subsectors."[36] The list of companies on the Dow Jones Islamic Index is growing as more businesses become involved and the U.S. government acts to approve and expedite the implementation of sharia finance.[37]

While the number of Muslims in the U.S. who are interested in Islamic financial products may still be relatively small, awareness of the Islamic financing methods is increasing steadily within the U.S. financial system. In 2009 there were 15 institutions with Islamic finance operations in the U.S., according to Maris Strategies. In that year, General Electric launched the first Islamic bond by a Western industrial company. GE has signaled that it will issue more bonds as it looks to attract new funds and wealthy individuals in the Middle East and Asia.

Currently, the most common form of sharia finance in the United States is sharia home finance, or mortgage-alternative products. Sharia mortgages were introduced in the United States in the 1980s. They grew slowly through the 1990s but then received a major boost when Freddie Mac and Fannie Mae started to back them in 2002. As a result of this backing, the number of sharia mortgages increased significantly. Today, sharia mortgages are available in 25 states, with the number of providers likely to expand further.

Restrictions on Christian mission and evangelism

Christian mission to Muslims is prohibited in many Muslim countries, and Muslims who have emigrated to the West often bring these attitudes with them. Although freely engaging in mission to Christians, Muslims often take great offence when Christians try to evangelize them.

In June 2010, U.S. citizens were arrested and jailed on charges of "disorderly conduct" for distributing Christian materials outside an Arab International Festival in Dearborn, Michigan. The incident gained public attention when footage was later posted on YouTube. Dearborn Police Chief Ron Haddad told the press that the arrests were to ensure security and to prevent festival patrons from being bothered. Dearborn, a suburb of Detroit, has one of the largest Arab Muslim populations of any city in the U.S.: an estimated 30,000 people.

Meanwhile, the case of teenage convert from Islam Rifqa Bary, who had to flee her family under what she alleges were threats of violence, shows some of the problems that converts from Islam can face. It is well established in Islamic law and societies that sane and unrepentant Muslims who leave Islam are apostates and, as such, deserving of death.

Islamism

Islamism (political Islam) became resurgent in the first half of the 20th century, developing from a movement of intellectuals into a mass international movement. Since the 1970s its spread has accelerated. Islamists aim at establishing Islamic political dominance across the world. They see the state as the best tool for implementing sharia. So they seek to gain power in the state and then use its coercive power to enforce sharia. Conflict is ongoing until this goal is reached, as "peace" is possible only under Islamic rule.

Islamism is at the root of the radicalization evident among Muslims in the West and across the Muslim world. Islamists have also developed programs for Islamizing Western society and its power centers in order to create an environment conducive to Islam.

For Islamists, Muhammad's migration from Mecca to Medina in 622 (the *hijra*) is a paradigmatic model for

Muslims to follow today. It is a flight from a region of persecution to a safe haven that is to be infiltrated and won for Islam, so as to serve as the launching pad for Islam's further expansion. Migration is thus viewed by Islamists as a stage in the political quest for the establishment of the ideal Islamic state.

To achieve their overall strategy, Islamists employ a variety of tactics in the West, including the U.S.

Dawa *(Islamic mission)*

Islamic mission, or *dawa*, is not limited to Muslim apologetics and efforts at converting individuals. Rather, *dawa* is very wide in scope, including efforts to convert whole societies. *Dawa* aims to establish Islamic-ruled states or enclaves that can serve as a compelling model to non-Muslims of Islam's power and benefits.

Johari Abdul-Malik, Director of Outreach at the prominent Dar al-Hijrah Islamic Center in Falls Church, Virginia, makes clear that Islamic *dawa* is very ambitious in its aims:

> Alhamdulillah [Praise to Allah] and we will live, will see the day when Islam, by the grace of Allah, will become the dominant way of life... I'm telling you don't take it for granted because Allah is increasing this deen [religion] in your lifetime. Alhamdulillah that soon, soon... before Allah closes our eyes for the last time, you will see Islam move from being the second largest religion in America – that's where we are now – to being the first religion in America.[38]

Formation of Islamic organizations

Organization is seen as a religious obligation by many Muslims, and Islamists have excelled at creating a vast network of interlocking organizations committed to spreading Islam in the West. The Muslim Brotherhood was founded in Egypt in 1928 by Hassan al-Banna (1906–1949). Emerging from the Salafi movement, it was the first of the plethora of Islamist organizations. Al-Banna aimed to seize political power by a gradual process, which began with education, recruitment and training.

Other networks such as the Jama'at-i-Islami, the Saudi Wahhabi-Salafi and the South Asian Deobandi organizations are all involved in Islamization activities both in Muslim states and in the non-Muslim world. These organizations join forces to create larger groupings and cooperative alliances, supported by various governments and intergovernmental Islamic establishments.

Pressure for sharia

Led by the Islamists, Muslim communities are demanding legal changes that would protect Islam and give it a privileged position in state and society. The demand for sharia in the West is expressed in areas such as food, marriage, divorce, politics, policing, hospitals, prisons, and banking, which (Muslims claim) should all be made more sensitive to Muslim religious customs and laws based on sharia.

Threat of violence

Another tactic the Islamists employ in order to further

their goal is to threaten (and at times carry out) violence. Among the most well known of these incidents are the fatwa against Salman Rushdie, the assassination of film director Theo Van Gogh in the Netherlands, and rioting in Muslim-majority neighborhoods of various countries in response to the Danish cartoons of Muhammad. When faced with such violence, or threats of violence, governments and individuals alike are cowed into conceding to radical demands. They start to censor themselves and avoid anything that might appear as criticism of Islam or Muhammad. Along these same lines, Islamic terrorism, an ongoing threat, is often portrayed by Muslims as being the "fault" of the West, an inevitable response to Western "provocation." And sadly, many in the West are quick to accept this interpretation of events.

The immense media influence of radical Islam means that Muslims anywhere in the world can be radicalized and provoked to violent action. A new generation of media-savvy communicators such as Anwar al-Awlaki, the Yemeni American cleric, is having a profound influence globally through their presence on the internet. Al-Awlaki is believed to have directly inspired many jihadists (particularly those in the West), thanks in part to his fluency in Arabic and English. Commenting on the attack by Major Nidal Malik Hasan on Fort Hood, he said:

> No scholar with a grain of Islamic knowledge can defy the clear cut proofs that Muslims today have the right − rather the duty − to fight against American tyranny.[39]

Islamist influence in the United States

The impetus for Islamic influence in the United States comes from two main areas:

Islamic groups and organizations

Firstly, there are Islamist organizations. These are generally part of broader networks such as the Egyptian Muslim Brotherhood. They include the Muslim Student Association and the International Institute for Islamic Thought (discussed above). Islamist organizations are adept at dominating Muslim communities, so that their message is pushed to the fore. Here is how one Muslim scholar described their impact in America:

> Thanks to their relentless activism, over time Islamists took control of many existing mosques and Muslim charities, and (again with the help of petrodollars) built hundreds of new mosques, religious schools, and community centers across the United States. Using tactics similar to the communists they organized domestic organizations to speak for American Muslims, making sure that their voice was the only one heard.[40]

Islamists in the U.S.A. have focused on organizations as a key part of their strategy. This was clear in a Muslim Brotherhood document.

> We must say that we are in a country which understands no language other than the language of the

organizations, and one which does not respect or give weight to any group without effective, functional and strong organizations.[41]

ISNA

The Islamic Society of North America (ISNA) is the largest Muslim organization in North America. It was established in the United States in 1981 at the same address as the Muslim Students Association (MSA). Muslim Brotherhood internal documents record, "[T]he Muslim Students Union (which soon became the MSA) was developed into the Islamic Society of North America (ISNA) to include all the Muslim congregations from immigrants and citizens, and to be a nucleus for the Islamic Movement in North America."[42] It hopes to achieve this aim by converting non-Muslims and strengthening Islamic sentiment amongst nominal Muslims. In a 1983 assembly, the ISNA recognized two priorities for Muslims in America: *dawa* and education.

ISNA is now an umbrella group that represents some 300 mosques, numerous Muslim organizations, and associations for youth, college students, and various professional fields. President Barack Obama's choice of ISNA President Ingrid Mattson, a Canadian convert to Islam, to offer an inaugural prayer in the National Cathedral is the second public association that he has had with an individual connected to the Muslim Brotherhood (al-Ikhwan) front groups. During Obama's campaign his outreach coordinator to Muslim groups, Mazen Asbahi, resigned after information was made public about his ties to Islamist and Muslim Brotherhood groups.

Thanks to Islamist organizations such as the ISNA, the Muslim Brotherhood has become hugely influential in America. In an October 2007 conference on the Muslim Brotherhood and the United States, Husain Haqqani, a professor of International Relations at Boston University, described the history of the American Muslim community up to the present. His conclusion defines the current landscape of Islamic organizations. "The mosques and organizations," he stated, "all ended up, or most of them ended up under Muslim Brotherhood control."[43] Haqqani, who now serves as Pakistan's Ambassador to the United States, wanted American policymakers and the public to recognize that "the Muslim Brotherhood created the networks that have dominated the U.S," and "most of the leading figures in the Muslim community ended up being people from the Muslim Brotherhood or people influenced by the Muslim Brotherhood."

In recent years other notable Muslim figures have also spoken about the extent of the Muslim Brotherhood's control of Islamic institutions within the U.S. They have warned of the Islamist movement's extensive, subversive influence throughout American political and cultural institutions. In a 2008 report on "The Muslim Brotherhood's US Network," Zeyno Baran of the Hudson Institute states, "[M]ost prominent Muslim organizations in America were either created by or are associated with the Brotherhood – and have therefore been heavily influenced by Islamist ideology." Muhammad Hisham Kabbani, a Sufi cleric and the founder and chairman of the Islamic Supreme Council of America, provided a similar assessment in a 1999 State Department forum. A well-organized Muslim movement of "extremist ideology," he stated "took over 80 percent of the mosques" in the United States.[44]

CAIR

The most prominent of the Islamist organizations in terms of media profile is the Council on American Islamic Relations (CAIR). CAIR works through "media relations, government relations, education and advocacy" and litigation to "promote a positive image of Islam and Muslims in America," and to "protect (the) civil liberties" of Muslims. The organization is headquartered near the U.S. capitol in Washington, D.C., and has 33 offices and chapters across the country.[45]

CAIR was established in 1994 by the Islamic Association of Palestine (IAP), an organization co-founded by Hamas political leader Mousa Abu Marzook. CAIR's attempted regulation of the critical discussion of Islamic issues in the American public square is focused on non-Muslims and on critics within the Muslim community. As one of the latter, the former publisher of Voices of Peace, Seif Ashmawy, has said, "It is a known fact that [both the American Muslim Council and] CAIR have defended, apologized for and rationalized the actions of extremist groups and leaders such as convicted World Trade Center conspirator Sheikh Omar Abdul Rahman, Egyptian extremists, Hassan al-Turabi, the Sudanese National Islamic Front, and extremist parliamentarians from the Jordanian Islamic Action Front and others who called for the overthrow of the Egyptian government."[46] Former FBI chief of counterterrorism, Steven Pomerantz, concurs, saying, "CAIR, its leaders, and its activities effectively give aid to international terrorist groups."[47]

Liberal Muslim organizations

It should be noted that a handful of organizations do represent a more liberal version of Islam. Unfortunately none has yet gained a significant following; however, they are putting up a brave fight to depoliticize Islam in America and thus deserve the support of Christians who are concerned about the impact of Islamism. Notable here is the American Islamic Forum for Democracy (AIFD), led by

Zhudi Jasser, a medical doctor in Arizona, which has made clear its opposition to Islamism in America:

> Current "major" Muslim organizations certainly deserve what is afforded to every political lobby in America. But as a political lobby, they subsequently lose the respect afforded to apolitical faith leaders in the United States. In a country which is founded upon the separation of religion and politics, they cannot be both. It needs to be made clear whether these organizations are representing a faith community or a political lobby. And make no mistake, the Islamist

political lobby is a part of the global ideological threat to the U.S. Once we see these organizations as political lobbies, then a critical quid pro quo about Islamism will be natural during meetings with our government. Other voices of anti-Islamism within the devout Muslim community will then be empowered rather than marginalized. Then, the greater Muslim community can actually begin to lead the charge against political Islam and its radical off-shoots.[48]

It is notable from this statement that liberal Muslims can be far more awake to the dangers of Islamism than their non-Muslim counterparts.

Saudi Arabia

The second key impetus for Islamist influence in the United States comes from Saudi Arabia. The Saudis have used their oil wealth to propagate the Wahhabi fundamentalist ideology through organizations such as the Muslim World League and have also sought to influence key Western institutions. They have visibly targeted American universities. The late King Fahd's nephew, Prince Alwaleed Bin Talal Alsaud, the 13th richest man in the world, with large stakes in Citigroup, Euro Disney, Fox, Four Season Hotels, and Saks Fifth Avenue, gave Harvard and Georgetown Universities $20 million each to be spent on Islamic studies.[49] They were by no means the first or only gifts. In the past, he has given to the Carter Center for Peace and Health Programs in

Africa and to the President George Herbert Walker Bush Scholarship Fund at Andover, Massachusetts. [50] A month after 9/11, he gave $10 million to Mayor Giuliani to rebuild the Twin Towers. However, Giuliani returned the gift after the Prince suggested that U.S. foreign policy had motivated the Towers' attack.[51] Other Saudi monarchies, according to Yale Daily News, have made contributions totalling $27 million to the University of Arkansas, the University of California, Berkeley, and Harvard University.[52] In addition to its efforts to control how Islam is taught and studied in the United States, Saudi Arabia has also directed ample funds towards far more sinister targets. According to the 2006 Department of State International Narcotics Control Strategy Report, "Saudi donors and unregulated charities have been a major source of financing to extremist and terrorist groups over the past 25 years."[53]

Security and terrorism

Islamists do not always restrict themselves to the gradual strategies of Islamization described above. While gradualist Islamists seek to work through the political sphere, violent Islamists focus on tactics that include terrorism, though the long-term goals of both gradualists and violent Islamists are essentially the same.

The attacks on American soil over the last decade are well documented and well known and do not need further discussion here. American security officials have frequently asserted that many more attacks are planned and thwarted than those that are actually successful.

It is alarming that so many Muslims in the West have become radicalized and have supported and engaged in jihad, both abroad and in the countries where they are living.

Undoubtedly part of the problem has been the success of Islamists in the Muslim community. They have managed to lay the groundwork for radicalization by pushing Muslims towards fundamentalism and anti-Westernism. Violence can be easily justified using sacred texts and historical sources. This creates a constant potential for radicalization. Younger Muslims living in the West may face a crisis of identity as they seek to combine Western and Islamic values and therefore are particularly vulnerable to radical ideas.

Conclusion

The multi-faceted challenge of Islam and Islamism has spread to almost every aspect of society and presents a major challenge to the West. Western governments are not showing sufficient awareness of the aims of Islamism and the tactics it is using as it seeks gradually to transform Western societies. The final chapter looks at how policy makers and leaders could respond to the challenges outlined here.

Lessons and Responses

This final chapter addresses the issues facing both Christian and secular leaders today. It highlights the problems both face due to the challenge of Islam and offers some suggestions as to how they can respond. The first chapter explored American identity and in particular the role of the church in America, discussing the challenges that American Christians are facing, particularly "hard secularism," multiculturalism and political correctness, which seek to undermine America's Christian identity. It also explored how these made both the Church and the West in general unprepared for the challenge of Islam. The second chapter showed that Islamic worldviews are fundamentally different from American and Western worldviews. The third chapter highlighted the challenge of Islam and of Islamism to the West, with particular reference to the United States. While it is clear that the West is faced with an epochal challenge, confusion still abounds as to how it should respond.

How Should Policy Makers React?

As already stated, most Muslims in the U.S. are peaceful

and have sought to assimilate within American society. But it must also be noted that there are forces currently at work that encourage Islam the religion to enter into the political space.

In broad terms, policy makers should continue to reassure the Muslim community in the U.S. that their presence is welcome and that their persons and their property will be protected. However, their religion and ideas must be subjected to the same criticisms and debate as Christianity and any other religion. Islam cannot be made a special case, immune from criticism or insult. It is not the duty of the state to promote a religion but simply to allow it to exist. Islam does not separate the sacred from the political; as a religion it wants to enter the public space. So policy makers must ensure that Islam can enter the public space only in the same way as Christianity and other religions do, that is, by virtue of their moral values. In other words, it is not the religion per se that should enter the public space but rather its values and virtues as expressed and lived out by its adherents.

Sharia, or Islamic law, can therefore have no place within the public sphere; nor can the more political expressions of Islam that hide under a religious burqa. The U.S. government must continue to affirm that the U.S. is not at war with Islam, but it must equally acknowledge when violence is perpetrated by practicing Muslims in the name of Islam. Therefore the religion and its ideology will have to be addressed. Another key issue for policy makers in the U.S. is how to stop radicalization taking further root within the American Muslim community.

Problems for Policy Makers in the West

Since 9/11, American policy makers have been grappling with how to approach Islam. This has proven to be a very difficult issue. Undoubtedly part of the problem is that policy makers have shown a lack of understanding or wishful thinking when they consider Islam. One of the most common errors is the desire to categorize Islam as two clearly separated types, one that is bad (usually al-Qaeda and terrorists) and one that is good (the rest of the Islamic world), and that the former is in fact an aberration of the latter.

George Bush made such a division when he spoke about the need to eradicate Muslims he labelled "Kharijis:" those who, he argued, represented the bad aspects of Islam. At the same time, he pursued a policy of friendship with other Muslims such as the Saudis, who, while not explicitly endorsing terrorism, were certainly responsible for exporting and cultivating fundamentalist forms of Islam.

Another important issue for policy makers is the question of protection and religious liberty for Muslims in America. Muslims are a very small minority in the United States and, as such, may on occasion need protection from overt discrimination or racism. Furthermore, the tradition of religious liberty for all is tightly bound to America's core identity. However, there is a tension. On the one hand, Muslims as individual citizens must be protected, as must their right to religious freedom. But should the state also seek to protect a religion or ideology? Protecting people and protecting ideas are two very different matters. Islam as an ideology needs to be challenged, not protected, especially when it is in the form of a strongly politicized Islamism involving the attempt to impose sharia on aspects of American life. Challenging this ideology while avoiding charges of racism or chauvinism is very difficult.

American leaders may remember the history of Catholicism in the U.S.A., which was initially treated with great hostility by American Protestants who feared it would subvert American identity and independence, especially after the great influxes of Catholic immigrants in the 19th century. However, Catholics adapted and were themselves shaped by American culture. Gradually they were embraced by the mainstream. However, as shown in the second chapter, the Islamic worldview and values are fundamentally opposed to the American worldview and values. This makes this process of (Catholic-like) adaption much less likely to occur. It also means there is always the danger that even those Muslims who seem to have embraced American culture may quickly become radicalized.

There is also an international aspect related to the fact that at the time of writing America is involved in two wars in the Muslim world and therefore requires Muslim allies. The war in Iraq has not achieved its objectives, and similarly the war in Afghanistan is not producing the hoped-for results. Since 9/11 American policy makers have become more aware of how volatile public opinion in the Muslim world can be and have recognized the need to reduce extremism and radicalization. The issue is further complicated by U.S. dependence on the Middle East for its vast energy needs. Furthermore, given the present state of U.S. finances, its need for employment and trade has made it increasingly dependent on the wider world, including the Islamic world, to achieve sustainability. These international factors have generally tended to encourage policy makers to respond to Islam in the most expedient way, which has involved viewing it through rose-colored glasses and seeking to avoid Muslim criticism at all costs.

This has particularly been the case with President Obama's engagement with the Muslim world and his Cairo speech. While it is positive that the U.S. is seeking to approach the Muslim world with a degree of humility, how far Obama has fully understood its worldview and attitudes remains to be seen. Seeking to find quick solutions to the Israeli-Palestinian problem, and believing that solving this would solve international terrorism, suggests a limited and naive understanding of Muslim thinking. Also, while there is a need for a Palestinian state, the question of Israel's security must be kept constantly in view, particularly in the light of a potentially nuclear Iran.

Responding to radical Islam

The attitudes outlined above have proven counterproductive when policy makers form policies to counter radical Islam. This type of policy-making requires first and foremost realism. It requires understanding of who the opponents are, what their strengths are, where they derive support and legitimacy, and their strategic goals. Wishful thinking has led to several misconceptions about radical

Islam and hence to a failure over the last decade to formulate effective policies to counter it.

Part of the problem for Western policy makers is that they have underestimated how long ideological battles last and how resilient ideologies can be, especially if they are grounded in culture and religion. A superficial understanding of how tightly bound Islamist ideologies are to Muslim populations has led some to claim prematurely that they have been defeated. In 2008 the then CIA director Michael Hayden claimed that there had been "significant setbacks for al-Qaida globally – and here I'm going to use the word 'ideologically', as a lot of the Islamic world pushes back on their form of Islam."[54]

However, al-Qaeda, and radical Islam in general, remain a significant (and in some places growing) threat:

- It is continuing to strike in the West and even on US soil
- It is establishing new bases (in Yemen, East Africa, and Pakistan) and consolidating existing strongholds
- It is recruiting new generations of young Muslims and Muslims living in the West

Just as there is confusion about what the terrorists' ideology actually consists of, there is also confusion about who the enemy actually is. According to President Obama's National Security Strategy, 2010: "We are at war with a specific network, al-Qa'ida, and its terrorist affiliates." However, this seems a rather narrow focus. What about the whole Islamist culture and ideology, which has the same long term goals as the terrorists, even though it does not always explicitly endorse terrorism?

As already stated, it is important to avoid giving the impression that the West is at war with Islam. But, on the other hand, to suggest that it is at war only with al-Qaeda is both misleading and counterproductive. The focus should be not merely on al-Qaeda, or even on the terrorist ideology that al-Qaeda promotes. The focus needs to be broader, including the wider Islamist ideology, which, though not always explicitly justifying terrorism, provides the ideological justifications for it by calling for Islamic dominance and a return to a purified form of Islam and by extolling the doctrine of jihad. This ideology not only emphasizes domination through violent means; it also strives for the peaceful or gradualist Islamization of all countries, through tactics that concentrate on every area of society, including the political, legal, social, media, and financial. The last chapter showed how this strategy is being worked out in the Western context.

Yet Western policy makers often seem intent on denying that there is any religious dimension to Islamism and Islamic terrorism. Ham-fisted judgments are passed by Western observers on terrorists' lack of Islamic legitimacy. For example, John O. Brennan, Barack Obama's assistant for Homeland Security and Counterterrorism, seems intent on emphasizing that jihad is a "legitimate term," and that Islamist terrorists have no right to use this term:

> Even as we condemn and oppose the illegitimate tactics used by terrorists, we need to acknowledge and

address the legitimate needs and grievances of ordinary people those terrorists claim to represent. Using the legitimate term jihad, which means to purify oneself or to wage a holy struggle for a moral goal, risks giving these murderers the religious legitimacy they desperately seek but in no way deserve.[55]

The problem with this type of misconception is that policy makers are happy to allow the continued influence of Islamism in Western societies and to help Islamists in the Muslim world, as long as they do not explicitly endorse terrorism. The outcome is that the Islamist ideology continues to dominate, both in the Muslim world and in the West, and Islamist networks continue to be a seedbed out of which terrorist groups originate, and with which they continue to exist in a symbiotic relationship. Policy makers try to minimize the problem of radical Islam by presenting it as having nothing to do with classical Islamic ideology, when in fact it has much to do with it.

Can approaches in the West change?

Clearly one of the main problems facing the West is a lack of clarity about what the Islamist ideology is, what its roots are and why it is successful. Not only is there is a war of ideas between Western approaches to Islamism, but also there is another war of ideas within the Islamic world itself about which type of Islam will be dominant.

A successful analysis of Islamist ideology must involve reading what the Islamists themselves are saying. Their self-definition can be very useful. It is important to be open to taking what Islamists say about themselves at face value. It is particularly useful to look at what Islamists wrote about themselves some decades ago, when they were very open about their aims and methods. They are now putting this into practice, even though many of their later writings may not be so explicit.

Old analytical habits are not sufficient to understand Islamist ideology. This phenomenon cannot be understood purely in terms of political motivations or of personality/psychological influences. The existing template for counter-ideology against totalitarianism does not function well in countering jihadism, owing to the religious element within jihadism, which is not a part of traditional analysis. Islamism and Islamist terrorism cannot be understood without identifying their religious core; and that core will not go away simply by our avoiding describing it in religious terms. Political correctness simply obscures the true nature of the ideology.

It is important to take seriously the ideology itself and to avoid the temptation to interpret the phenomenon of radicalism wholly as a "response" to Western behavior. Policy makers should beware of being distracted by issues of "perception" as opposed to substance. They must understand that Islamism has an internally coherent motivator of its own – its religious ideology.

Clearly religion has returned to international relations, and this must be recognized by policy makers. The politicization of religion and the sacralization of politics is a particularly dangerous mix in the case of Islam, owing to the faith's compounding of *dín wa-dawla* (faith and state) and its universalist, global pretensions. The vocabulary of politics is entirely changed and needs to be understood at face value; it is far more than simply adding a cultural identity to a conventional struggle. It is necessary to recognize Islamism as a rooted and determined ideology, and not to fear criticism for taking this approach.

Countering Islamization in the West

While countering radical Islam across the world requires vigilance and clear thinking, Western governments must also be aware of attempts to Islamize Western societies from within. Policy makers, therefore, must become aware of the threat of Islamism and the attempts to Islamize Western institutions. Even demands that, on the face of it seem relatively benign, such as Muslims seeking "Islamic finance," are in fact part of an overall process of transforming Western societies. Islamists are constantly putting pressure on Muslim-minority communities to demand more and more privileges.

The excessive demands of Islamists must be rejected, along with their blaming of host societies for all the difficulties faced by Muslims. It is crucial that democratic Western societies do not give up their hard-won heritage of equality before the law, freedom of expression and freedom of religion. It must also be made clear that tolerance must work both ways and that threats of violence are unacceptable. Muslim communities must try much harder to isolate and expose Islamists who reject integration and the violent radicals among them.

Reform in the Muslim World?

Localized threats involving radicalized Muslims throughout the world will not be solved unless problems that derive from global Islam are solved. Undoubtedly Muslim governments, religious leaders, and intellectuals are far more influential in the Muslim world than any of their Western counterparts. It is their voices that resonate amongst Muslim communities across the world. Western policy makers cannot hope to influence the Muslim discourse with their opinions about who is an authentic Muslim, because their opinions carry little weight. The war against Islamist ideology will probably be won or lost by Muslims. Western policy makers can hope only to influence and support those who are trying to undermine the ideology.

The battle to reform Islam and undermine the Islamist ideology will by no means be quick or easy. Weaknesses in the ideology exist, but they are not easy to exploit. The Western worldview assumes an uninhibited exchange of ideas. Ideologies, theories, and the wildest of hypotheses and speculations can be given free rein in a society based firmly on freedom of belief and freedom of speech. A corollary of this is the ease with which many Westerners can abandon former beliefs or guiding principles and move on to embrace new ones. This process causes relatively little or no anguish, let alone a crisis of identity, in a culture of free discussion and debate. But in Islamic culture, individuals are more firmly wedded to their ideologies and beliefs and to their history.

Nevertheless, it is clear that there is potential for a change in approaches to the Islamic sources, which could lead to a genuine ideological change in the Muslim world. A good example of this can be seen in the case of Mansour al-Nogaidan, a Saudi journalist and former Salafi, who has instead embraced Sufism (Islamic mysticism):

> Muslims are too rigid in our adherence to old, literal interpretations of the Koran. It's time for many verses – especially those having to do with relations between Islam and other religions – to be reinterpreted in favor of a more modern Islam. It's time to accept that God loves the faithful of all religions. It's time for Muslims to question our leaders and their strict teachings, to reach our own understanding of the prophet's words and to call for a bold renewal of our faith as a faith of goodwill, of peace and of light.[56]

Al-Nogaidan goes on to call for reform throughout the Muslim world, focused on reinterpreting the texts:

> I see what Islam needs – a strong, charismatic personality who will lead us toward reform, and scholars who can convince Islamic communities of the need for a bold new interpretation of Islamic texts, to reconcile us with the wider world.[57]

A minority of Muslims are bravely defying traditional and Islamist concepts in order to reinterpret Islam in
a way compatible with modern concepts of secularism,
individual human rights, religious freedom, and gender
equality. They represent a wide variety of approaches to
the challenges of modernity. Most see themselves as good
Muslims who accept a core of basic Islamic values, distilled
from the Muslim source texts, and they believe that those
basic values ought to determine all contemporary interpretations of Islam. However, they are willing to ignore traditional concepts and interpretations that contradict modern
values of freedom and equality. They see a need radically
to change traditional, orthodox Islam in such a way as to
integrate liberal, humanistic values at its very core. Others
go further and see themselves only as culturally Muslim,
having rejected Islam as a religious system. These include
Muslim humanists, agnostics, and atheists. All demand the
inculcation of pluralism and of democratic freedoms in
Muslim societies. Such developments offer a glimmer of
hope for the long-term future.

Policy makers must be alive to the potential for change
in the Muslim world, yet aware that they have limited
scope to influence these developments directly. But they
must certainly avoid supporting those Islamists and traditionalists who are seeking to undermine any liberal reform.
Every interaction with the Muslim world must be calculated
to support liberal reformers and undermine Islamists.
Currently this is far from the case, and Western governments will often sacrifice the long-term benefits of support-

ing liberal reformers in return for the short-term benefits of supporting Islamists.

How should Christians react?

As discussed in chapter 1, Christians can have a pivotal role (especially in America) in influencing the way in which the challenge of Islam is approached.

Protecting America's Christian identity

Undoubtedly Christians have to respond to broader challenges in society that threaten fundamentally to undermine America's Christian identity. American Christians face a variety of challenges from hard secularists, multiculturalists and those pursuing politically correct agendas. The long-term aim of these forces is completely to remove any Christian influence from the public square and reshape American identity in a post-Christian mould. Sometimes they are willing to complain about "offense caused to Muslims" or "discrimination against Muslims" or "Islamophobia" as a way of furthering their own agenda and restricting Christianity. Christians therefore face a challenge as they engage in the public square; they will need great wisdom in order not to play into the hands of their opponents yet still to be assertive in continuing to proclaim America's Christian identity and emphasize its Christian heritage.

Without becoming complacent, American Christians can take comfort that their country is very religious and that American Christianity remains much more prominent than its European counterpart. Ninety-two percent of Americans still believe in a god and 63% believe that one or more sacred texts are divine revelation. In America, 40% of the population regularly attends church services; in Britain the figure is as low as 2%.

Using reason

The battlefield in Islam has always been over reason. In the 8th century the conflicts between the Mu'tazilites and the Ash'arites centred on whether the Quran was created or uncreated. The Mu'tazilites, who argued that it was created, appealed to reason to support them. They were defeated by the Ash'arites who rejected reason and argued for the primacy of revelation. Pope Benedict XVI has pinpointed this as the pivotal area that contemporary Islam needs to address.

For Christians, reason came to the fore in the Enlightenment. Although one can note the devastating effects this had in subsequent centuries, particularly with the rise of liberalism within Christianity, yet on the other hand reason allowed societies to be built without revelation (real or reputed) dictating the content of law, so they did not become tyrannies or totalitarian states. Reason enabled recognition of many of today's fundamental freedoms, the freedoms of the intellect, the freedoms of commerce and politics and, in the modern era, the freedom of individual human rights. These freedoms are rooted in the Biblical view of humankind: in the *imago dei* of creation, and in the incarnation and redemption of Jesus Christ.

Despite this heritage, reason is once again coming under fire from extremist religious forces in our modern world, not only Islamic forces but also from other religions, including Christianity. Reason is also under fire in that honest debate is increasingly being prevented, as both political correctness and fear take root in Western societies.

But reason is God-given, and it is a vital tool in responding to the challenge of Islam. How different the world might be today if the Mu'tazilites rather than the Ash'arites had triumphed. And now there is another chance to re-visit that debate and perhaps to enable reason to win this time. Christians must not shy away from reason. They must separate their emotions from their minds, and recognize that they can critique the religio-political system that is Islam while still loving the people who follow it, Muslims.

Being careful about interfaith dialogue

The Church must preach love for all Muslims as human beings created in God's image and for whom Christ died. It should certainly not preach hatred of Muslims. But neither should it be naive as to the nature of Islam and its objectives in the U.S. and about what is happening in the Muslim world; nor should the American Church fail to support the suffering Church in the Muslim world. The Church must recognize that Islamist terrorists are much more than a miniscule fringe group and have legitimacy within Islam. The violence perpetrated by such groups is rooted both in the ideology of large contemporary Islamist movements and in the traditional, orthodox and classical version of Islam, especially its doctrines of jihad, *dawa* and dhimmitude, and also the law of apostasy, presented in the authoritative Islamic scriptures and commentaries. Most of the religious leaders (clerics) represented in the interfaith dialogue process represent this classical form of Islam in its many local varieties (Sunni, Shi'a, Wahhabi, Islamist, etc.). Any interfaith dialogue with Muslims must address these problems and demand visible action rather than mere declarations of goodwill.

The love of Christ drives His people to preach the Gospel to all, including Muslims, and it casts out all fear, including fear of Muslims, Islam or its effects. It follows that the Church should both fund and support evangelism to Muslims in many countries and also take seriously the plight of Christians in Muslim lands and the plight of converts from Islam to Christianity.

In a globalized, shrinking world, and especially in contemporary Western multi-ethnic and multi-religious societies, it will be necessary for Christians and Muslims (and all others, including religious and non-religious people and atheists), as good citizens, to have conversations and to cooperate for the common good in community or national matters of shared concern. In such common ventures Christians must ensure there is a clear understanding of equal commitments and definite boundaries. Such cooperation must never be at the expense of Biblical convictions in order to gain the goodwill of the Muslims involved. It must not assume the equal validity and moral equivalence of Islam and Christianity. Certainly it must never signify that Christianity is an archaic part of a superior Islamic tradition, nor remove the Christian imperative for mission.

Finally the dangers of the political pressures in the dialogue movement must be fully realized. Christians should not offer themselves as pawns to powerful governments or parties aiming at purely political advantage. While Muslims endorse the unity of religion and state, Christians must always remember Christ's warnings against such manipulation.

Emphasizing religious liberty

Christians across the Muslim world face discrimination, harassment or outright persecution and do not enjoy the religious liberty and equality that is taken for granted in the West. Christian converts from Islam are particularly vulnerable in Somalia, Afghanistan, Saudi Arabia, and Iran, where they are likely to face either death or imprisonment. Christian minorities living in Egypt, Nigeria, Pakistan, and Indonesia face other challenges, whether physical attack or injustice and discrimination. Christians living in the Muslim world can only dream of having the rights and liberties that Muslims living in the West enjoy, although some Muslims in the West would suggest that they face discrimination in key religious matters, including their desire to live by sharia. Few Christians living in the Muslim world can freely evangelize, and for many of them building churches or even meeting to worship invites harassment. While the imperative of unconditional love requires Christians to seek the welfare of the other, it is increasingly important also to address the issue of reciprocity. For in a globalized world, how far is it acceptable that Muslims in the West should enjoy the freedoms that their co-religionists elsewhere deny to others?

Christians should be encouraged to place pressure on Muslims to demand that Christian minorities living in Muslim countries enjoy full religious liberty. Pressures to stop evangelism among Muslims must be vigorously resisted. Muslims should be encouraged to reform Islam, annul the apostasy laws and condemn the persecution of Christians and converts from Islam.

Seeing the rise of Islam in spiritual terms

For Christians the growing presence of Islam in the West has to be seen in the context of God's providential dealings with the nations and the Church. In this light it can be seen as both a possible warning of a coming judgment and as an opportunity for mission.

- Some would see the rise of Islam as a warning of a coming judgment on the West that has rejected God, the Gospel of Christ, and its Christian and Biblical heritage and turned to post-modern relativism, materialism, atheism and neo-pagan immorality. As Europe faces the dangers of accelerating Islamization, terrorism and jihad, as long-fought for freedoms and rights are being lost, it would seem that God may be saying, "Repent or worse is yet to come."

- The rise of Islam is an opportunity for a lukewarm Christianity that has lost its doctrinal and evangelistic edge. As Christians see Muslim zeal, commitment, and willingness to sacrifice, they should be driven to repent, pray for revival, and act boldly for God in this generation. God is testing the faith and loyalties of His people, who need to stand firm on their Biblical foundations, beware compromises and syncretism, and reach out in love to Muslims, offering them the Gospel of salvation in Christ. Mission and witness to Muslims are to be encouraged, and the suffering Church in Muslim states should be prayed for, supported and defended.

Battling for truth

C.S. Lewis wrote of "the doctrine of objective value, the belief that certain attitudes are really true, and others really false, to the kind of thing the universe is and the kind of things we are."[58] As discussed in chapter 3, Islam is deliberately manipulating the truth by re-writing history. Given that Islam permits its followers to lie in a number of specific situations, one of which is the defense of Islam, this is likely to be no mere passing phenomenon, but a continuing one. How can Christians counter this, particularly in the intellectual sphere? In practical terms, what can they do to set the record straight and make the truth known?

The relativism embedded in the modern secular American worldview is another challenge to truth. Relativism has become such a dominant feature of the West today that

Pope Benedict speaks of the "dictatorship of relativism." Relativism developed when post-war America drifted towards pluralism, a pluralism that now embraces every ideology that exists. This pluralism gave rise to relativism, which in turn has led to an existential emphasis on experience rather than on objective truth. As C.S. Lewis commented, people "are simply not interested in the question of truth or falsehood. They only want to know if it will be comforting, or 'inspiring', or socially useful."[59]

Re-establishing Christian principles and virtues in society

Relativism is rooted in the primacy of the individual. While focusing on the individual can have many positive aspects, it can also lead to a rampant individualism without any restraint. Experience, which is so highly valued in a relativistic worldview, becomes the touchstone of reality, of morality, and of spiritual truth, which includes the rejection of moral absolutes. This in turn leads to narcissism, the worship of self, pleasure as the highest goal, a focus on economic well-being and consumerism, the rejection of moral absolutes: in short , to what Pope Benedict describes as a life lived as if God did not exist. How can American Christians reverse this trend in their society?

To give one practical example: countless films and TV programs reflect the ideals of secular humanism as opposed to the ideals of a society based on a Christian values. Should Christians mount a campaign to complain or boycott the most extreme of these? Or should they accept this as part of the persecution that Christians are called to undergo?

Christians face not only the challenge of relativism but also the opposing challenge of Islam. Pope Benedict has spoken of "the eclipse of God" in our modern society. The vacuum created by secularism, individualism and relativism is increasingly being filled by Islam, because Islam rejects pluralism and embraces absolute truth (as Muslims see it), with no window for relativism to operate. The individual is subsumed into the community, and community values and loyalties are central. Experience is irrelevant (except in Sufism, and even the Sufi are bounded by Islamic theology, morality and practices).

It was almost half a century ago that Harry Blamires, a friend and student of C.S. Lewis at Oxford University, stated that there is no longer a "Christian mind."[60] His comment is one Christians should be earnestly reflecting on in the 21st century. How do Christians in a secular, post-modern society, where Islam is active and growing, reshape the secular worldview to which so many Christians have succumbed, in order to develop a Christian worldview, in effect a Christian mind?

On a strategic level, how also can Christians affect the public sphere, whether in law, economics, medical sciences or any other field of human endeavor, while at the same time avoiding the development of a theocracy? Leading Islamic thinkers are confidently and creatively seeking the transformation of society according to Islamic principles, an Islamization process that would, if unhindered, lead ultimately to a theocratic Islamic state. As salt and light, cannot Christians transform our societies according to Christian principles?

Remembering the transcendence of God

Islam's disciplined rejection of relativism issues from its emphasis on God's transcendence, making pleasure subservient to duty. "Islam" means submission: submission to the ultimate, to the transcendent and merciful god of Islam. The Muslim is a submitter, effectively a slave of the divine, living out his or her life in conformity with the divine will, the sharia. The god of Islam, having created the world, resumed his seat on his throne, leaving the world to itself. His interventions are arbitrary and without moral consistency or personality. This Islamic view of the divine is at best deistic.

Is this another area in which Christians should respond to the Islamic challenge, by refocusing their faith, by remembering the transcendent in the Christian faith? Islam at this point offers a potential corrective to Christians who have increasingly replaced divine transcendence with divine immanence, leading to a faith based on experience and feelings, increasingly devoid of holiness or any sense of awe and majesty, where God is nothing more than a pet or buddy who stands alongside and helps when possible. God is a Person, who has revealed Himself to us as God made human. This God is both divine and human, transcendent and immanent. Christians must affirm His immanence and rediscover His transcendence to give a better balance to their own faith.

Christians in the U.S. are faced with two further dangers in terms of God's transcendence. One is to acknowledge His transcendence and then say, "So what?" believing that every individual is free to do whatever he or she wishes to do. The other is to manipulate God's transcendence to satisfy our own gratification and personal whims. As Mr. Beaver says of Aslan, the Lion and Christ-figure in The Lion, the Witch, and the Wardrobe, "Course he isn't safe. But he's good. He's the king, I tell you." Aslan is not a tame lion.

Conclusion

Pessimism has begun to take root among segments of American society, which hitherto has been particularly optimistic. As discussed in chapter 2, pessimism is a fruit of scientific materialism and the general focus on technology. This, coupled with America's economic woes, its changing role on the world scene, and its newly revealed powerlessness to effect the changes it desires in other countries, has led to a manifestation of pessimism that surprises many outside observers. For the Muslim, all things are predetermined. The god of Islam wills what he wills. Christians rejoice to know that the Lord, our Creator, Redeemer and Sustainer, is in control, that He knows the end from the beginning, that they have confidence and hope in placing their lives in His hands. They know there is what Aslan called "a Deeper Magic from before the dawn of time." They believe in an End, where the crucified Christ will return victorious as the Lord of Glory. They are not filled with the fatalism of

Islam but rather with the hope of the Christian Gospel, and it is that which must drive them forward in a spirit of hope and optimism to face today's challenge.

Endnotes

1   C.S. Lewis, *An Experiment in Criticism*. Cambridge: Cambridge University Press, 1965, pp. 137-138.

2   Wayne Martindale and Jerry Root, eds., *The Quotable Lewis*. Carol Stream, Illinois: Tyndale House Publishers, 1990, p. 22.

3   Throughout the text "America" refers to the United States of America.

4   Arthur Schlesinger, *The Disuniting of America: Reflections on a Multicultural Society*. New York: W.W. Norton & Company, 1992, p. 134.

5   Samuel M. Zwemer, Editorial, *The Moslem World*. Volume VII, 1917, p. 2.

6   http://www.isna.net/Documents/Root/ISNATruth Document.pdf, p. 8.

7   "Islamic Europe?" *The Weekly Standard*, October 4, 2004, http://www.weeklystandard.com/Content/Public/Articles/000/000/004/685ozxcq.asp (viewed November 1, 2010).

8   Akbar Ahmed, *Journey into America*. Washington, DC: Brookings Institute Press, 2010.

9   Art Moore, "Did CAIR founder say Islam to rule America? Muslims confront Omar Ahmad as newspaper stands by story," *WorldNetDaily.com*, December 11, 2006, http://www.wnd.com/?pageId=39229 (viewed November 1, 2010).

10   "Overwhelming Majority Oppose Mosque Near Ground Zero," *CNN Politics*, August 11, 2010, http://politicalticker.blogs.cnn.com/2010/08/11/overwhelming-majority-oppose-mosque-near-ground-zero/ (viewed November 1, 2010).

11   Raymond Williams, *Keywords: A Vocabulary of Culture and Society*. New York: Oxford University Press, 1985, p. 87.

12   U. S. Department of Defense, *Dictionary of Military and Associated Terms*. Washington, D.C., 2005.

13   James Truslow Adams, *The Epic of America*. New York: Blue Ribbon Books, 1931.

14 *Tawhid* is the unity of God, a basic theme of Islamic theology, as described further on in this section.

15 S. Abdullah Schleifer, "Understanding JIHAD: Definition and Methodology - Part One," The Islamic Quarterly, London Third Quarter 1983, http://www.salaam.co.uk/knowledge/schleifer1.php (viewed November 1, 2010).

16 M.A. Zaki Badawi, *The Reformers of Egypt.* London: Croon Helm, 1978, pp. 48-49.

17 Abu Dawud, *Hadith* no. 4278.

18 Yusuf al-Qaradawi, http://www.islamonline.net/fatwa/english/FatwaDisplay.asp?hFatwaID=61551 (viewed August 10, 2005).

19 Egdunas Racius, *The Multiple Nature Of The Islamic Da'wa*, http://ethesis.helsinki.fi/julkaisut/hum/aasia/vk/racius/themulti.pdf, p. 116 (viewed November 1, 2010).

20 "Muslim Americans: Middle Class and Mostly Mainstream," Pew Research Center, May 22, 2007, p. 9.

21 Ryan Mauro, "Muslim Enclaves U.S.A.," *Frontpage Magazine*, July 9, 2010, http://frontpagemag.com/2010/07/09/muslim-enclaves-u-s-a/print (viewed November 1, 2010). See also Daniel Pipes, "Permit Muslim-only Enclaves?", http://www.danielpipes.org/blog/2004/08/permit-muslim-only-enclaves, August 27, 2004 (viewed November 1, 2010).

22 See Eat-Halal.com, http://www.eat-halal.com/qanda.shtml.

23 Zabihah.com, http://www.zabihah.com/.

24 See IFANCA, http://www.ifanca.org/index.php.

25 Dominique Patton, "Malaysia Looking for Bigger Role in Halal Industry," March 22, 2006, http://www.meatprocess.com/Industry-markets/Malaysia-looking-for-bigger-role-in-halal-industry (viewed November 1, 2010).

26 Greg Folinazzo and Melissa Furkalo, Halal Beef Study: Report on Findings, August 2005, Agri-Trade Service, http://www.ats.agr.gc.ca/sah/4078-eng.htm (viewed November 1, 2010).

27 Faruq Abdul-Aziz v. Newark Police Department, 3rd Cir. 97-5542, March 3, 1999, http://caselaw.lp.findlaw.com/cgi-bin/getcase.pl?court=3rd&navby=case&no=975542p (viewed November 1, 2010).

28 Zeinab Ali v. Alamo Rent-A-Car, 4th Cir, 00-1041, March 6, 2001, unpub., http://pacer.ca4.uscourts.gov/opinion.pdf/001041.U.pdf (viewed November 1, 2010).

29 Salina Khan, "Employers Adjust to Muslim Customs: Ignorance, Not Prejudice Cited in Cases," *USA Today*, June 25, 1999, 12B.

30 Guy Rodgers, "Fethullah Gulen: Infiltrating the U.S. Through Our Charter Schools?" Act for America, http://www.actforamerica.org/index.php/learn/email-archives/1069-fethulla-gulen-infiltrating-us-through-our-charter-schools/ (viewed November 1, 2010).

31 From the official website of Ismail al-Faruqi, http://www.ismailfaruqi.com/news/dr-ismail-al-faruqis-approach-to-islamization-of-knowledge/.

32 See quote on IIIT homepage, http://www.iiit.org/AboutUs/Agreements/ICRD/tabid/109/Default.aspx. *Din al-fitrah* means the religion of the intrinsic human nature, i.e. Islam, which is the natural religion of humans before they are spoiled by their parents and environment and made to follow other religions.

33 James Beverly, *Islamic Faith in America*. New York: Facts on File, Inc., 2003, p. 83.

34 Geneive Abdo, *Mecca and Main Street: Muslim Life in America After 9/11*. New York: Oxford University Press, 2006, p. 188.

35 Daniel Roselle, *World History*: A Cultural Approach. Harlow: Ginn, 1976.

36 Dow Jones Islamic Market Indexes, Overview, http://www.djindexes.com/islamicmarket/ (viewed November 2, 2010).

37 For more on this subject, please see, e.g., Patrick Sookhdeo, *Understanding Shari'a Finance*. McLean, VA: Isaac Publishing, 2008.

38 Andrew McCarthy, "More Moderate Muslims: For a preview of the Ground Zero Mosque, check out Virginia," *National Review Online*, August 7, 2010, http://www.nationalreview.com/articles/243635/more-moderate-muslims-andrew-c-mccarthy (viewed November 2, 2010).

39 http://www.defensestudies.org/?p=1008.

40 Hedieh Mirahmadi, "Navigating Islam in America," p. 50, http://www.worde.org/articles/navigating_islam_HM.pdf (viewed November 2, 2010).

41 "An Explanatory Memorandum On the General Strategic Goal for the Group In North America, 5-22-1991," p. 12 [a strategy document approved by the (Muslim Brotherhood) Shura Council and the Organizational Conference for the year 1987], www.investigativeproject.org/documents/case_docs/445.pdf (viewed November 2, 2010).

42 Internal document of the Muslim Brotherhood (HLF Trial Exhibit: Bate # ISE-SW 1B23/0002005).

43 Rod Dreher, "Haqqani on Muslim Brotherhood's real agenda," *Dallas Morning News*, December 2, 2008, http://dallasmorningviewsblog.dallasnews.com/archives/2008/12/haqqani-on-musl.html (viewed October 28, 2010).

44 Islamic Extremism: A Viable Threat to National Security," An Open Forum at the U.S. Department of State, January 7, 1999 (Islamic Supreme Council of America transcript).

45 See http://www.cair.com/AboutUS/VisionMissionCorePrinciples.aspx.

46 Steven Emerson, *American Jihad*. New York: The Free Press, 2002, p. 222.

47 Daniel Pipes, "Reply to CAIR's Attack on Daniel Pipes," http://www.danielpipes.org/cair.php (last viewed November 2, 2010).

48 M. Zuhdi Jasser, "Our Government's Dangerous Partnering With the Wrong Muslims," Family Security Matters, February 2, 2007, http://www.familysecuritymatters.org/publications/id.95/pub_detail.asp (viewed November 2, 2010).

49 "World's Billionaires," *Forbes Magazine*, March 27, 2006; Saudi Arabia had 11 billionaires in 2006.

50 Eliana Johnson, Untitled, *Yale Daily News*, January 17, 2006, http://www.yaledailynews.com/news/2006/jan/17/_-31286/ (viewed November 2, 2010).

51 "America Recovers: Giuliani Rejects Saudi Prince's Gift," CNN manuscripts, October 12, 2001, http://transcripts.cnn.com/TRANSCRIPTS/0110/12/se.10.html (viewed November 2, 2010).

52 Eliana Johnson, Untitled, *Yale Daily News*, January 17, 2006, http://www.yaledailynews.com/news/2006/jan/17/_-31286/ (viewed November 2, 2010).

53 2006 International Narcotics Control Strategy Report, State Department, 333, http://www.state.gov/p/inl/rls/nrcrpt/2006/vol2/html/62145.htm/ (viewed November 2, 2010).

54 "U.S. Cites Big Gains Against Al-Qaeda," *The Washington Post*, May 30, 2008.

55 White House Briefing, August 6, 2009, remarks by John Brennan, Assistant to the President for Homeland Security and Counterterrorism, to the Center for Strategic and International Studies (CSIS), subject "A new approach to safeguarding Americans,"http://www6.lexisnexis.com/publisher/EndUser?Action=UserDisplayFullDocument&orgId=574&topicId=25188&docId=l:1018813300&start=6 (viewed November 2, 2010).

56 Mansour al-Nogaidan, "Losing my Jihadism," *Washington Post*, July 22, 2007, http://www.washingtonpost.com/wp-dyn/content/article/2007/07/20/AR2007072001808.html (viewed 2 November 2010).

57 al-Nogaidan, "Losing my Jihadism."

58 C.S. Lewis, *The Abolition of Man*. New York: Macmillan, 1947, p. 29.

59 C.S. Lewis, "Modern Man and His Categories of Thought," in *Present*

Concerns: Essays by C.S. Lewis. New York: Harcourt Brace Jovanovich, 1986, p. 65.

60 Harry Blamires, *The Christian Mind: How Should a Christian Think?* Ann Arbor, MI: Servant, 1963.

About the Author

Patrick Sookhdeo gained his Ph.D. from the University of London's School of Oriental and African Studies in the UK. He has also been awarded a D.D. from Western Seminary, Portland, Oregon, for work on pluralism, and a D.D. from Nashotah House Episcopal Seminary, Wisconsin, for work on human rights and religious freedom.

Dr Sookhdeo is International Director of Barnabas Aid, a Christian agency that gives practical assistance to Christians around the world who suffer discrimination, oppression and persecution on account of their faith. He is also Director of the Institute for the Study of Islam and Christianity, a research and training organisation focusing on Christians in Muslim-majority contexts and the challenges of Islam to the Church and society. He is a widely acknowledged authority on Islam.

Dr Sookhdeo is the author or editor of more than fifteen books and has taught and lectured at many academic institutions in the U.S.A. and elsewhere. He has been Adjunct Professor at Western Seminary and Visiting Professor at the Reformed Theological Seminary in Orlando, Florida and Washington DC. He has served as co-ordinator of various international missions committees and conferences, and acts as a consultant on contemporary Islam to government, business and the media. He is Dean-Theologian of Abuja Diocese of the Anglican Church of Nigeria.

Dr Sookhdeo received the Spring 1990 Templeton UK project award to an individual for work in the community, the 2001 Coventry Cathedral International Prize for Peace and Reconciliation, and the St Ignatius Theophoros' Decoration as Commander (the most senior award of the Syrian Orthodox Church).